Praise for *Ask More, Get More*

"Michael Alden recounts his poverty-laden upbringing . . . His struggling single mother . . . jostled for food stamps and begged to keep her son and herself from eviction . . . Alden's story . . . motivates and educates.... Whether you're rich or poor, content or striving, *Ask More, Get More* has golden nuggets of information sprinkled from cover to cover . . . a must read!"

—*John Abdo, Olympic Strength & Conditioning Coach, 1976, 1980, 1984, and 1988 Olympic Games, Master Fitness Trainer, National Fitness Hall of Fame Inductee*

"*Ask More, Get More* teaches anyone from any background not only how to make money, save money, and create wealth, but how to be successful in any aspect of life."

—*Jim Shriner, best-selling author of* Live Disease Free to 103

MICHAEL ALDEN

ASK MORE, GET MORE

HOW TO EARN MORE, SAVE MORE, and
LIVE MORE . . . JUST BY ASKING

EMERALD
BOOK CO.

Published by Emerald Book Company
Austin, TX
www.emeraldbookcompany.com

Distributed by Emerald Book Company

For ordering information or special discounts for bulk purchases, please contact Emerald Book Company at PO Box 91869, Austin, TX 78709, 512.891.6100.

Design and composition by Greenleaf Book Group LLC
Cover design by Greenleaf Book Group LLC

Cataloging-in-Publication data
Alden, Michael, 1975-
  Ask more, get more : how to earn more, save more, and live more—just by asking / Michael Alden.—1st ed.
    p. ; cm.
  Issued also as an ebook.
  ISBN: 978-1-937110-60-4
  1. Self-realization. 2. Success--Psychological aspects. 3. Negotiation. I. Title.
BF637.S4 A43 2014
158.1   2013949507

ISBN 13: 978-1-937110-60-4

Part of the Tree Neutral® program, which offsets the number of trees consumed in the production and printing of this book by taking proactive steps, such as planting trees in direct proportion to the number of trees used: www.treeneutral.com

TreeNeutral®

Printed in the United States of America on acid-free paper

13 14 15 16 17 18   10 9 8 7 6 5 4 3 2 1

First Edition

To the most important person
in my life,
my little girl, Morgan.
Daddy loves you!

CONTENTS

Acknowledgments

Thank you to my friends and my family for their continued encouragement. I would not be who I am today without their support. I also thank my dedicated and talented editor Chris Benguhe, without whose support this book would not be what it is today.

INTRODUCTION

Thank God, I was born poor. I would not have wanted it any other way. Growing up poor was actually a gift; a gift that is very difficult to see when you are growing up. After all, how can living in constant fear of being homeless, having your electricity shut off, and eating from food pantry shelves be considered a gift? How can standing in the special free food lunch line or going to school early to get state-sponsored breakfast for twelve years be a gift? How can growing up in a neighborhood that was surrounded by crime, violence, and drugs be a gift?

Growing up poor taught me the value of money and hard work. Growing up poor taught me how to save, share, and be generous. Growing up poor caused me to yearn for more. The way I grew up may have been tough, but there are many worse situations than mine. I was never homeless, but often had the fear of being evicted. I never went hungry, but we had to improvise, adapt, and find ways to eat. I never had a Christmas without gifts or a special treat, but many of our holidays were subsidized by a charitable organization or completely funded by the Salvation Army. As a young child, I watched my mother struggle and cry trying to figure out how to get by. I used to listen to my mother negotiate and beg the Housing Authority not to evict us. I remember once when my mother's old, beat-up Dodge Colt was repossessed and she had to negotiate more money than it was worth to get the car back. You get the picture: I was poor—not the poorest of poor, but certainly below the poverty level and poor enough to qualify for government-subsidized housing, food stamps, and state cheese.

Growing up poor forced me to learn how to use what I had within me to make more out of life. And as far back as I can remember, I have always worked.

Growing up in New England, we always expected a few snowstorms in the winter and blistering hot days in the summer. I was so excited when it snowed and school was cancelled. Even at age nine, I got up early, grabbed my shovel, and walked door-to-door to shovel driveways in what I thought were the rich neighborhoods. Depending on the day and the amount of snow, I partnered with a friend and we'd either split up or do the driveways together to cover more houses. I literally worked from 7:00 a.m. to 7:00 p.m. or even later. And on a good snow day, I'd come home with one hundred dollars in my pocket! When other kids were building snowmen, I was out hustling driveways. If I grew up middle class or rich, would I have done the same thing?

During the summers, I set up a lemonade stand on a busy street that was close to my house and solicited people driving by. Sometimes I got lucky, and a jogger or walker passed by. They almost always bought a cup of lemonade. One summer I franchised my business and we had three stands surrounding the neighborhood close to my house. We took turns riding our bikes back and forth to replenish the lemonade, and I learned the important concept that the direct, concerted effort of many is much more powerful than that of just one person.

At the age of ten, I dreamed of owning a cool BMX bike with all the accessories—chrome rims, cool brakes, and flashy colors. But these types of bikes—GT, Redline, or Haro—cost a minimum of $300. I saw kids in my neighborhood riding around on these kinds of bikes, knowing full well that they stole them. If I wanted to keep my integrity, for me they were unattainable.

My uncle, Buddy, worked as a janitor at a Pontiac dealership in Danvers, Massachusetts, and every week or so he brought me giant bags full of aluminum soda cans worth five cents a piece. All I had to do was bring them to the redemption center and get the money. I forget what a big bag was worth, but it was probably around five or ten dollars. I think my mom gave me the idea to save that money for the bike I wanted. I thought it was a great idea, and not only did I save, but then I went out and found more cans. I picked cans out of barrels; I asked family members to save cans; I went on hunting excursions . . . and then I discovered that a two-liter soda bottle was worth ten cents! *Ten cents!* That was awesome, and I hunted for them on a daily basis to get pocket change to buy things like candy or baseball cards. Over time I was able to buy that bike. I was so proud; it wasn't stolen, and it wasn't a gift. I bought it with the help of Uncle Buddy. It had magnum green fluorescent wheels and all of the chrome accessories a bike could handle. And that bike, well . . . it also made me a lot of money, as you shall read.

When I was ten, I got a paper route and kept it through middle school, picking up new customers every week. The paper route was a tough responsibility. It had to be done every day and the papers had to be delivered before 4:00 p.m. My customers expected to see the "unwet" paper on their doorstep when they came home from work. When school ended at 2:00 in the afternoon, I rushed home and got on my BMX bike to deliver my papers. I was just beginning to get involved in sports and had to be very disciplined with my time so I didn't miss practice for football, baseball, or basketball. Finally, I would get home and do my homework (sometimes). The paper route wasn't a super profitable venture, but I made a decent amount of money; I cleared about fifty dollars a week, which was not bad for a kid living in the projects. I learned to appreciate the value of hard work and the almighty dollar. Many times my mom needed to "borrow" my money, and I remember being a bit annoyed since I had worked so hard. Looking back, I can barely comprehend how my mother managed and am glad I was able to contribute.

Eventually, I gave up the paper route because sports and school were more important. During the summers of my early to mid-teens I began a mini landscaping business. I had about four or five regular customers who paid me ten to fifteen dollars to cut their lawns. I invested most of that money back into new equipment. I scoured neighborhoods, looking for old lawn mowers people had thrown out that I could fix. I remember buying my first weed whacker (also known as a hedge trimmer) and thought it was the coolest thing ever. I dreamt of running my own landscaping company. At fourteen, I had two or three lawn mowers, some hedge clippers, and a couple of weed whackers, and every summer I hit up my regular customers for more work.

When I got more tools I offered additional services like trimming hedges. Though trimming hedges wasn't as profitable as mowing lawns, it allowed me to charge for a new service and increase my cash flow.

Finally, sports and my grades took over, and at fifteen I realized that my grades were not where they were supposed to be. To be honest, I was also getting in trouble and hanging out with the older kids from my neighborhood. Although I had other jobs, I knew that in order to make it out of the neighborhood, I needed more than drive. Later on I will discuss other areas in my life that helped me learn how to harness the traits we *all* have inside: traits that enable us to achieve our goals while getting the most out of life.

I tell these stories to provide some perspective on my background and help *you* realize *you* have the same skills, the same opportunities, and the same abilities and drive within *you*. I was lucky that I was forced to find a way to get the things I wanted in life by finding honest ways to make money at a very young age. *Ask More, Get More* isn't an autobiography, however; it is a book that shows *you* that we all have within us the same drive, skills, desires, and abilities to get more out of life, just by asking. And not only asking others, but asking yourself questions that will harness the power of the human genome and spirit beyond what you thought possible.

When reading *Ask More, Get More*, don't jump ahead or skip any part of the book. Cleanse your mind of all assumptions, knowledge, and judgment. Embrace the thought that you are willing to apply these principles and techniques in your life. And then apply them with enthusiasm each day. Don't say, "Oh, I knew that," "that is stupid," or "that won't work." If they were stupid and didn't work or if you already knew all these strategies and techniques then you must be an extraordinarily successful individual. Therefore, as a successful person, you will appreciate the refresher course on some of the skills you may have forgotten (we all do).

INSANITY

Most people do the same thing over and over every day and expect a different result; yes, they say that is the definition of insanity. Well, you are most likely not insane if you have this book in your hands. All of us suffer "temporary insanity" at some point in our life. I have been working out since I was twelve years old, and being of the mesomorph body type, I am considered a "big guy." I played football, baseball, basketball, and soccer, among other sports, for most of my life—some better than others. But after I graduated college, I realized that I didn't need my football weight anymore. I kept doing my same football workout for a few years and ate the same way . . . and I couldn't lose the weight. Finally, around age twenty-eight, I did the Body for Life Program. It changed my thinking about exercise and nutrition, even though I already "knew" most of the concepts and strategies. I knew the techniques were simple and easy. However, one very profound thing I learned from Body for Life was that if you can't be honest with yourself, then who can you be honest with? If you lie to yourself and say that you dieted properly, or that your intensity level was at a ten when you know it was at a five, then you are lying to yourself and ultimately hurting yourself. So, I constantly ask *myself* questions—the same questions you will learn to ask yourself and others throughout this book.

Once I applied the strategies I learned in Body for Life, I lost more than thirty pounds and had visible abdominal muscles for the first time in my life. Now, fast-forward to the age of thirty-six. I am in a physical rut. I "go" to the gym almost every day. I have a trainer. I try to "diet" and do all the things that I was doing in the past. I still cannot lose weight. I am also an avid reader of magazines like *Muscle and Fitness* and *Men's Health*, and yet I still cannot lose weight. In fact, I am/was at my all-time high in tonnage! So, rather than doing the same thing over and over again and expecting different results, I mix it up. I try something new. I added—and am now addicted to—yoga . . . any type. And I have lost weight, improved my muscle tone, posture, and mental clarity, and ultimately feel great.

Just by purchasing this book you have made the decision to

change your habits, change your thoughts, change your life, and cure yourself of the "temporary insanity." As I have said on television, many of these techniques are simple, *easy*, and effective. Of some you will say, "Well, that is ridiculous," or "it's just too easy," or "what's the catch?" The fact is—there is no catch. Many of the *Ask More, Get More* principles you may have "heard" or "knew about," but you just didn't do them for one reason or another.

I was in one of my first "hot" yoga classes—out of my element, exhausted, sweating, a bit delirious due to the rapid loss of electrolytes—wondering if I belonged in the class. The instructor said something profound when describing a basic yoga move and its effectiveness for core strength. "Simple things work only if you do them."

Let me repeat: Simple things work, but only if you do them.

So enjoy the book page by page, chapter by chapter, and once you finish you will have internalized the principles of *Ask More, Get More* and you will have in your brain the skills that many people only think they have. You will not only have these skills, you will know how to recognize them and, better yet, how to use them. You will notice that there are margins in this book where you can and should take notes. There is significant research that confirms that when you write something down, you will have better retention. When I read, I am constantly underlining text and writing notes. Also, there may be a few words (only a few) new to you or that you may not understand. Don't skip over the word. Look the word up at Dictionary.com—they even sound out the word for you. If you are reading this book on the Kindle, iPad, or any other tablet, many of them have features that allow you to highlight the word and get the definition quickly.

The *Ask More, Get More* techniques work, some faster than others, and they are easy to implement and simple to understand. I cannot emphasize enough: these principles, strategies, and techniques are simple and easy *and they work*! You just need to do them! So smile, and be excited. Get more out of life just by asking and doing things that we all can do. Tap into the skills we all have within.

PART I

ASK MORE FROM YOURSELF

CHAPTER 1
ASK YOURSELF TO THINK DIFFERENTLY

*If you properly use your imagination it will help you convert your
failures and mistakes into assets of priceless value; it will lead you to
discovery of a truth known only to those who use their imagination;
namely, that the greatest reverses and misfortunes of life often open
the door to golden opportunities.*

—Napoleon Hill

WHAT MAKES YOU SO DIFFERENT? NOTHING.

My mother is HIV positive, my stepfather died of AIDS, my father
was addicted to cocaine, both of my grandparents on my mother's
side were hard-core alcoholics, and my brother Dominic spent most
of his life "locked up" and eventually died of a drug overdose. One

of my other brothers spent a majority of his youth behind bars for offenses that range from drug possession to armed robbery. Another brother was in rehab for a heroin addiction, and a close friend I grew up with is in jail for life for first-degree murder. Sounds horrible, doesn't it? Why have I had success? Why was I able to graduate high school, go on to college and then law school, have a successful career as a lawyer, and then become the CEO of a very successful marketing firm that generates millions of dollars?

People always ask me, what makes me different? How did I "make it"? Well, if you were to analyze our DNA, nothing would be different between my family members and me. What is really different is the way I think. That's it. I am not smarter than any other person. I was not lucky, and I wasn't given anything other than opportunity. Some would argue with me and say things like, "Well so and so had a disability, their DNA showed," or *blah, blah, blah* that inhibited their success.

Now here is the good news. My mom is doing great, and she is an inspiration. She was diagnosed almost thirty years ago but is still going strong. My father is also doing very well. He overcame a drug addiction and never looked back. My brothers are also finding their way and are destined for great things.

My intention here is not to shine a light on my own greatness or success—just the opposite. I am pointing out that if a schlub like me from a crazy family like mine (and I say that with love) can make something out of himself and have the kind of life I dreamed of having, then so can you!

I am no different than any other human being. I am far from perfect and, like everyone else, I have lots to work on, but I have programmed my mind to think differently, to *ask* questions in order to get more out of life. I want more out of life, and I am sure you do too. You just need to *ask,* and *more* will come!

IMAGINATION: one of the most powerful tools that humans have to help us visualize our dreams and goals.

Imagination is our ability to form mental images and concepts in our brains to foster ideas and turn our goals into reality.

"SO YOU WANT TO BE A CRIMINAL?" HOW I USED TO THINK—AND WHY I CHANGED

When I was at the pivotal age of fifteen, some thought of me as the poor kid who was also a punk. Some also thought of me as a troublemaker who was getting involved in criminal activity: stuff like shoplifting, fighting, and just being a bad kid.

My father many times would have me stay at his house on the weekends, even when I was fifteen. One weekend he took me to the beach and as we were walking he turns to me and says, "So you want to be a criminal?" He said it like a father might ask, "So you want to be a doctor?" I was shocked and didn't understand why he asked that. He then said, "Well right now, the things you are doing would put you into the class of a wannabe criminal and just a punk." He said if I wanted to continue to do what I was doing then we should make sure I was good at it. I was in complete shock. He told me he could introduce me to some people he knew: people who were actual gangsters, drug dealers, and other unsavory characters.

He then went on to describe what my life would be like. I would be constantly looking over my shoulder, maybe carrying a gun, and most certainly be in and out of jail. He *asked* me if I was prepared to be shot at, possibly killed, and most certainly incarcerated.

Recently I was working in my dad's garden, and I asked him if he remembered that talk. He said of course he did. I told him that that conversation changed the way I saw my future. I looked into the life he described and realized that it was not what I wanted. I thanked him for changing the way I thought about where I wanted to be in life at the time of that talk and in the future.

Whether you are someone who is in trouble with the law, not happy with your current living situation, or dissatisfied with your employment situation, *ask* yourself, where you sit today: What does your future look like if you keep doing what you are doing? Are you happy with the end result? If you are not happy, then the good news is that no matter what the situation is, you can change it.

MY BEST FRIEND AND HOW HE CHANGED HIS LIFE

But I say again: Do not put me up on some kind of pedestal because I was able to change my life. My best friend has a pretty amazing story as well. In fact it's astonishing that we are even friends at all, considering how we met.

When I was in eighth grade, I was jumped by a bunch of kids from the other side of my town. There were about four or five of them against me. The police came, the aggressors were arrested, and some were put into protective custody. One of them was a kid my age; his name was Kevin. Kevin grew up in very similar circumstances to mine, just in a different neighborhood. He hung around with bad kids, got into fights a lot, and was going down the wrong path. We were not friends and did not like each other at all. But we came to have something very important in common.

The day after the fight I was at home and there was a knock on my door; Kevin and his mom were standing on my front steps. As you can imagine, I was reluctant to open the door. But I did, and Kevin and his mom came into my house. Kevin's mom made him apologize, and she said something that was prophetic. She said, "Shake hands, and who knows? Maybe you guys will be best friends someday." We didn't agree but both shook hands.

Kevin went to the trade school within my high school. Trade-school kids were in a different wing of the high school and were also looked down upon by the other students. They didn't take regular classes and were considered dumb. Kevin was considered by many as a tough guy who was not the brightest bulb on the tree. I also thought that.

After we graduated high school, Kevin enlisted in the military. We always kept in touch, and Kevin had a successful career in the military. While I was in college Kevin was protecting our country. What Kevin learned in the military was invaluable; he learned that not only was he not dumb, but he was extremely smart. Whenever he could, he took classes while in the military to make himself better. After his service Kevin enrolled at the local community college. The interesting thing was that Kevin not only went full time, but actually took seven classes one semester. Kevin got straight A's for those two years of community college. The "dumb kid" from the trade school knew he was smart, but most everyone else didn't. After graduating, Kevin was *encouraged* by Harvard to apply for admission. Harvard! I remember talking with Kevin about it. It was surreal: the tough-guy, trade-school kid was now considering Harvard! Well, after much thought, Kevin ended up going to Northeastern in Boston because they had a strong criminal justice program. Kevin is now a very successful police officer in New York. He teaches firearms safety and tactical classes. Kevin, too, is no different than anyone else. He just decided he was going to think differently. Kevin made the decision that he wasn't going to succumb to negative thoughts and give in to what others perceived him to be.

Kevin's mom was right; Kevin and I became extremely close in high school, and to this day I consider Kevin my best friend. The tough trade-school kid who was also going down the wrong path knew he could be more, and that's exactly what he did. Kevin *asked* more out of himself, and that's what he got: *more*. More than anyone thought possible—and he just *asked*.

EMBRACE YOUR IMAGINATION AND IMAGINE WHAT *YOU* CAN HAVE—JUST ASK!

Have you ever heard someone say, "Oh, don't mind him, he has a vivid imagination," or "He has an overactive imagination"? Though there are many factors to success, I can't stress enough the importance of *imagination*. Your imagination is one of the most powerful tools available to the human mind. Encourage imagination, embrace it, and utilize it. There is no such thing as an overactive imagination.

Imagine this—what if Leonardo DaVinci's parents told him he should stop imagining things? Or what if Steve Jobs was told to stop imagining a better computer? Do you think we would have the *Mona Lisa* or the iPad if their imaginations were suppressed? Leonardo DaVinci built a robot in 1495. *1495!* Steve Jobs modestly said he has never invented anything, he just imagined a better version of what was already out there. There were hundreds of MP3 players on the market before the iPod, but which device revolutionized the music industry? As a result of the iPod, the iTunes store was created and literally changed the way we listen to and pay for music.

When I was in fifth grade we built one of Leonardo's inventions: a parachute that looked like an inverted pyramid. It seemed like a ridiculous contraption and most certainly wouldn't work. But that didn't matter; we learned about gravity and the thought process behind building it. After we completed it we had the opportunity to stand on the roof of our elementary school and let it go to see what would happen. We had also made a traditional parachute to compare the utility of each. The point is, our imaginations ran wild as we thought about possibilities—the sky was the limit.

We always hear the phrase "think outside the box," which simply means use your imagination. I can't tell you how many times we've brainstormed creative and imaginative ideas that propelled our business ventures at my company. We solved so many challenges not by looking at our schooling, at our transcripts in school, or at our SAT, LSAT, GRE, or any other standardized test score, but rather by focusing our collective imagination to solve challenges and grow our business.

But most of all we force ourselves and others to see ourselves and our company as a success in every venture; we refuse to accept any other outcome.

WHAT IS CONTRARIAN THINKING? AND HOW CAN IT HELP YOU?

In case you haven't already figured out who I am—or, I should say, who I was—I was the kid who should have ended up in jail or dead. In fact when I was sixteen, my girlfriend's mother told me that's how I was going to end up. Maybe she said that to motivate me. But to be honest I don't think that's why she said that; I think she believed it.

Regardless of her intentions, that comment bothered me and has stuck with me to this day. That is what people thought of me! Jail or dead? Well I became determined to defy them and their predictions about me. And so I did whatever I could to change. I started to ask for more in the way I thought and the way I lived.

My cumulative grades in high school were horrible. My SAT scores were barely enough to allow me to play sports *if* I got into college. But, around the age of fifteen, I started to change the way I thought and also to change my social circle. It was a gradual process, and I had many missteps.

But when you look at my transcripts, you can see a gradual increase in my grade point average, and eventually there were a lot of A's and B's. I went on to be elected senior class president and captain of my football team. Due to my commitment to my academics coupled with my extracurricular activities and the support of my family and teachers, I was fortunate enough to get accepted into a couple of colleges. I eventually chose Springfield College, the place where basketball was invented, the YMCA principles were espoused, and where Dr. Seuss lived—the famous author who not only changed my life as a child but impacted the lives of millions of other children. Coincidence? I'm not sure.

When I first got into college it was a bit of a culture shock, and to be honest I wasn't sure if I belonged. But I told myself that I *did* belong and that I wasn't going to let *myself* down along with the countless other people who gave me the *opportunities* that ultimately opened the door to college. I had a decent undergraduate academic record, was respected by my peers and professors, and went on to be class president for three years before going to law school. I did all this by taking what you might call a contrarian view.

CONTRARIAN THINKING

A contrarian is defined as a person who takes an opposing view, especially one who rejects the majority opinion, as in economic matters. The first time I heard the word "contrarian" was about two years ago when I was interviewing my good friend Dean Graziosi about his new real estate program. My infomercials are in an interview-style format similar to that of Charlie Rose.

Dean said, "When people are worried about the real estate market, they should think more like a contrarian." I had never heard the word and I just nodded my head and agreed with him. After the cameras were off, I asked him what it meant. He explained that his whole life, people told him not to do things because they didn't make financial sense to them. These people would say things like, "The real estate market is crashing; why would you buy real estate in this economy?" Dean just thought a little differently, and it has paid off for him.

Now in my advertisements on television for *Ask More, Get More* I take shots at real estate programs sold on television and say they are not easy. I point out that they work for a limited number of people, and I still stand by that statement. However, the difference between Dean Graziosi and many other so-called real estate gurus is that he *really* does this stuff. Every day he is actually buying and selling real estate and has done so for almost twenty years. If after reading my book, you want to dive into the real estate investment world and learn Dean's strategies, then go to www.deangraziosi.com and check out his program. I have met his students, and many have made a lot of money. Or if, after reading this book and going to Dean's site, you are really interested, go to my website, AskMore-GetMore.com, for a special discount on all of Dean's products and services.

Dean taught me something I already knew; I just didn't know the word for it. In order to be successful in life, you can't always go with the masses and do what you are supposed to do. During the Great Depression Howard Heinz, of the H. J. Heinz Corporation, built more factories, hired people, offered medical benefits, added product lines, and expanded outside of the United States. It was a bold move, and many questioned the decisions he made, but today Heinz is one of the largest companies in the world and sells more than just ketchup.

I am in no way in the same class as Heinz, but many times I make decisions or come up with ideas that some would say are crazy. I have found that in order to be successful, you have to think differently. It is more than thinking *big*; you have to ask questions that others consider crazy or stupid. But if you don't ask questions or push the boundaries you will never know the limits.

FORTY HOURS A WEEK

Arlen, a Brazilian in his mid-thirties, who cleans my office, speaks broken English. My office is roughly 20,000 square feet, and he is here seven days a week—my office is *always* clean. You can eat off the floor in my bathrooms. Many times when I am at the office at night, I enjoy talking with Arlen. He is *always* here, no matter what. Now, the interesting thing about Arlen is that he has a full-time job delivering supplies for a company that sells everything from gravel to sand and loam. One day he came into my office with a big smile on his face and said, "Hey, Mike, how many hours you think I had last week?" I asked, "At your other job?" and he said, "Yeah," so I guessed, "Seventy-five."

I was close; he worked *seventy-seven* hours the prior week, plus he was at my office *every day*.

I asked him why he had so many hours of overtime, and he told me it was because he was a producer. He went on to tell me how the other drivers don't like him, because they are paid hourly and don't understand how he outproduces them week in and week out, based on a forty-hour week. He told me that he averages twenty deliveries a day, while everyone else achieves ten or eleven a day.

I then asked how he did it. He said he maps out his routes and finds the fastest way to get to the point of delivery. The other drivers take the *long* way, because they are paid hourly and they are content with just getting paid for forty hours a week. He then told me, "Even though I'm paid hourly, if I can make my deliveries faster, then my employer will give me more hours." So, rather than thinking only about his forty-hour pay, he is thinking about how to get more hours. He does it, not by milking the forty hours and just doing the minimum, but by finding a way to get his work done faster, become more valuable to his employer, and thus make *double* what all of his fellow drivers make.

Even though he is being paid overtime, Arlen is more valuable to his employer, because he doubles the number of deliveries. By making more deliveries faster, he not only makes his employer more money, but the clients receiving the shipment are more productive. Arlen thought just a little differently—and doubled his compensation!

"I'M GOOD ENOUGH. I'M SMART ENOUGH.
AND DOGGONE IT, PEOPLE LIKE ME."

—*Stuart Smalley,* Saturday Night Live *fictitious character*

THE POWER OF POSITIVE THINKING

There are books, courses, articles, tapes, videos, and everything in between about the *power* of positive thinking. Thinking in a positive manner can boost your health, your wealth, and your life. It is a scientific fact that maintaining a positive attitude improves your life. But how can you do such a thing when you are living in a shelter, unemployed, have no prospect of employment, or if your current situation seems impossible to extricate yourself from? How can you think positively if you feel like you are underappreciated at your job or seem to always have speed bumps in your way? How can you think positively if every time you seem to move one step forward, someone else is pulling you two steps back? How can you think positively if you are sick, injured, or somehow handicapped?

You just do! Your thoughts do *not* control you; *you* control your thoughts. When you realize that *you* are in control of your mind, then you will realize that the thoughts *you* put into your head are what will determine your future.

A lot of the books and tapes out there go on and on about the importance of positive thinking. I could probably cover a couple of hundred pages myself with stories about how positive-thinking people are almost always successful. Everybody gets down; I know—I do too. I am human, and I can certainly be a grouch (ask my amazing assistant), but I remind myself of the indisputable power of the mind and its effect on everything around me.

I met a woman named Ellen in yoga a while back who reinforced with an exclamation point what I already knew. I was running late for the class and I noticed that a woman in her mid-forties was also trying to get to the door before it locked for the duration of the class—and the woman was wearing an oxygen tank! My first thought was that there is no way this woman is going into a Bikram Power Yoga class. It is 100 degrees and 100 percent humidity.

I was wrong. For an entire hour this woman, with an oxygen tank, performed some of the most difficult poses the instructor offered. I was humbled and amazed. But perhaps her ailment was temporary or slight asthma, I thought. So after the class, I asked, "How do you do this class with an oxygen tank?"

She responded enthusiastically, "Honey, I was supposed to be dead six years ago!"

So of course, I asked, "What do you mean?"

She went on to tell me how she was diagnosed with a rare disease called lymphangioleiomyomatosis, or LAM. LAM is a rare disease that basically forms tumors all over the lungs, effectively destroying them; there is no cure and no understanding of the cause of the illness. I had never heard of LAM before, but I asked her how she did it.

And she said, "Because *I know I can*, I am going to live, and *I know I can do this*." She was so positive and vibrant. Her story is inspiring. But there are Ellens all over the world, and the only explanation for her survival is the power of positive thinking.

I have a very dear friend, Jim, whose wife has suffered with rheumatoid arthritis since the age of sixteen. This debilitating autoimmune disease is degenerative and causes severe pain. Her name is Julie, and she is an amazing woman. She lives her life in constant pain, has had multiple surgeries, and has even faced amputation of her foot due to the severe pain. I do not see Julie all that often, but a few years ago we all went to the Red Sox game, walking from bar to bar before the game and having a few beers along the way. Keep in mind, this woman is in severe pain with every step, but she not only walked with us, she stood up in crowded bars, smiling, making jokes, and having a good time. Her husband, Jim, is one of the most positive people I know, though as I type this, Julie's health is failing due to the drugs she is forced to take to just allow her to function.

When I asked Jim how she does it, he said, "We just get up every day and thank the Lord for what we have, and look forward to the day." They maintain a positive attitude. Jim and Julie are two amazing people who always think positively despite how hard life may be.

At the start of this section, there is a quote from Stuart Smalley, a fictional character on *Saturday Night Live*. With Stuart, *SNL* was essentially making fun of the power of positive thinking. Stuart would look into the mirror and say, "I'm good enough, I'm smart enough, and doggone it, people like me."

But I learned from the immortal Zig Ziglar that what Stuart Smalley did *works*! In Ziglar's book *See You at the Top*, he suggests doing the following exercise every morning when you wake up: *clap your hands* and say out loud, "Today is going to be a terrific day, I am not going to make excuses, and I will not give up."

I'M MAGNIFICENT, BUT I WILL GET BETTER

I do some business with Zig Ziglar's nephew, John Ziglar. We speak often on the telephone and every time I ask him how he is doing, he replies in his jolly Southern accent, "I'm magnificent, but I will get better." He has trained himself in the habit of projecting to others that he is magnificent. When most people hear that response, they are taken aback, as they don't expect it. Now, John has not had an easy go at business; he has struggled like many of us during this tough economic time, but no matter what the situation he always responds the same way—*magnificent*.

I was on a conference call the other day with the CEO of a huge, billion-dollar nutrition company, and to be honest, I was a little nervous when I first realized he wanted to speak with me. But, when he called me and asked me how I was, I responded by saying, "Fabulous, but it's only 11:30; I will get better." He laughed and said, "Great." This was the first time I spoke with this man and we only spoke for about ten minutes, but he ended the call by telling me he wants to do business with my company. When people ask me how I'm doing, I say, "Fantastic, fabulous, wonderful!" It really throws people for a loop. But, it trains my subconscious mind to feel fantastic and to have a fantastic day. It is also infectious—the person who asked the question smiles, which helps them feel better. Then, hopefully they will have a better day.

A couple years ago I was at the home of a very successful businessman. This man made millions of dollars and his house was magnificent. Imagine 10,000 square feet, seven bedrooms, ten bathrooms, a four-car garage, and every toy imaginable. I used one of the many bathrooms, and there I found taped on the mirror a piece of paper that looked like it had been there for years. This paper had the following list written on it:

› I am going to have an amazing day.

› I am going to be successful.

› I am worthy of my success.

› I will achieve anything I set my mind to.

I don't know if those four things have any particular significance to this person, but the fact is this dog-eared piece of paper with its handwritten list of four phrases meant something to him. I have on my desk my own motivational phrases that I look at every day. I do this because I know that successful people before me have done the same. I encourage you to do it, too.

So now that you know one of my trademark secrets, when you are asked how you are doing, respond in your own way by saying something positive like, "I'm terrific, magnificent, wonderful." I do it all the time. Every day when you wake up, clap your hands with enthusiasm and say, "Today is going to be a terrific day, I am not going to make excuses, and I will not give up." Do this *every day*!

"IT ISN'T THE PEOPLE YOU HIRE
WHO WILL MAKE YOUR LIFE MISERABLE;
IT'S THE PEOPLE YOU DON'T FIRE."

—*Harvey Mackay*

CLEANSE YOUR SOCIAL CIRCLE

When I was a kid, I sometimes crossed the line between what was right and wrong with my ruffian friends. But I was lucky. My elementary school was a wonderful (though unintentional) social experiment. The school was located in an area that had some of the town's most affluent kids and also the poorest kids—like me. I was always getting in trouble, but I took notice of the more affluent kids and realized I wanted what they had. I didn't want to be embarrassed about my living situation; I wanted nice clothes and an unsubsidized lunch. The social diversity at my elementary school, and even in my middle and high school, gave me a glimpse into the world of possibilities. I didn't know exactly how I was going to get there, but I knew that one day I was going to achieve a higher standard of living. What I didn't realize then, at least consciously, was that achieving that dream would be a result not only of the things that I did or didn't do, but it would also depend on the actions of the people I chose to surround myself with.

When I was about sixteen my life changed forever when a friend in the neighborhood made a decision that took the life of a young girl. This decision ruined his life as well as many others. When this tragic murder happened, I was dating a girl who was upper middle class. She had the things I wanted—a nice house and a car. Her dad was a doctor, which allowed her family to live comfortably. I, on the other hand, was still flirting with the line between right and wrong. Right around this time, sports became a very important part of my life and I became friends with other athletic kids from the more affluent parts of town.

The boy who made the horrific decision to take someone else's life did not see the opportunities that I saw and was not taking advantage of school activities or sports. Because of his poor choices, I made the decision to distance myself from him, and we were no longer close friends. One summer day, he asked me to go for a walk with him and a group of other boys, and something inside of me said not to. Fortunately at that very moment, my well-off girlfriend drove by my neighborhood and asked me to go out with her. That day, this sixteen-year-old friend murdered his fourteen-year-old girlfriend and was ultimately sentenced to life without parole. One event, one choice changed my life forever.

Still, I wasn't out of the woods. I was trying to escape the neighborhood circle of bad boys I grew up with, but this murder brought me back in, and the media and others lumped all of the kids from my neighborhood into one basket. The media unjustly crucified us as *all* bad kids, even though by the time the case went to trial, I was class president and captain of the football team. I had to testify in court, and what I testified about was not good, since I saw a lot of bad things when I was a kid. The district attorney at the time was attacking me personally in the paper. I didn't understand why; I was just a kid.

But many of my peers, teachers, family members, and coaches came to my aid, and the district attorney realized what he had done was wrong. Coaches and teachers wrote to the local paper in my defense, and it was wonderful to read what they thought of me and my character. This was such a difficult time for me, but I was fortunate to be able to discuss this horrific situation with many of my coaches and teachers. Their message was clear; they all told me that I had great potential and that this was the time to cleanse my social circle. Following their advice, I decided to quit hanging out with kids or other people who were a negative influence.

Fast-forward to my career, and the same lesson rings true. One of the most difficult but important things I have learned about in business is having to fire people. I don't know many people who actually enjoy the act of letting an employee go. But if you don't make the tough decisions, your business suffers and, in some instances, fails. When it pertains to your personal life, you must do the same. In order to grow personally, professionally, and spiritually, you need to fire the negative people around you.

FRIENDS

A friend is someone you can trust and whose opinions and companionship you value. You can define what friendship means to you, but for me, the preceding phrase describes a friend. Several years ago, I had a momentous day. I had set a goal of *purchasing* a Rolex Submariner with a gold and steel band and the blue face. It is a very expensive watch, and it was a goal that I had set several years prior to the purchase. I, of course, used my phrase that I will mention later in this book and got a great deal at a real Rolex dealer. I was so excited; a kid who grew up with nothing, I now had on my wrist something worth more than some people make in a year. It was a goal I achieved.

That night I met up with a couple of high school friends of mine who were upper to middle class. They had grown up in my town and were both college educated. We met in a smoke-filled club and ordered a couple of cheap drinks while I showed them my watch. They looked at it and made comments like, "A watch doesn't define me," "I can tell time just by looking at my cheap twenty-dollar watch," and "A Rolex isn't going to make you a better person." All of these were valid comments, but each one was negative.

I tried to tell them that it was a goal I set for myself, and I had achieved my goal. As they sat on their bar stools in a smoke-infested club, surrounded by old men who could have been somebody, I realized that I could no longer hang out with these guys.

It's not that they are bad people—I still consider them good friends—but in order for me to be successful I need to be surrounded by people who also want to be successful. They were not trying to rain on my parade or be downers, at least not consciously. They were just conditioned by their surroundings to be this way. I realized that I had to cleanse myself of these acquaintances. Now, just to be clear, cleansing your friends doesn't mean you have to expel them from your life forever, but depending on the level of their negativity and potentially destructive behavior, you just stop hanging out with them. It doesn't mean you can't be where they may be, and you may even still talk with them, but you have to realize that socializing with negative people, friends or not, for extended periods of time can harm you and potentially infect you with "excusetosis," a disease I will talk to you about in the next chapter.

I tell you this story not to disparage my high school friends but rather to get you to look at your circle of friends and ask yourself if they are bringing you down. If they are, you need to distance yourself from them—*now*. Do not get infected with diseases such as procrastination, excusetosis, and failure.

I have only a few close friends and many associates, or "people I know." The associates are people I grab a drink with here and there. My true friends are confidants and successful in their world. Your friends do not have to be wildly successful people, but they need to be people who won't bring you down.

An interesting fact about one of the guys in the preceding story is that he has completely changed his life and his way of thinking. He is much more positive, he is physically in great shape, he changed what he eats, and also no longer drinks any alcohol. I now enjoy speaking with him; he has embraced positive thinking and now sees that he too wants more out of life than hanging out in smoke-filled rooms with has-beens.

WHAT ABOUT THOSE CRAZY FAMILY MEMBERS?

Unfortunately for me and for many others, sometimes the people we need to fire are family members. Now, let me be clear: *family* does come first, but that does not mean you need to be around family members all the time. You may find that in many instances it is a family member or even the entire family circle that brings *you* down.

When my family reads this book I'm sure they will say things like, "Well, that wasn't me," or "I always knew he would make it," in order to make themselves feel better. The truth is I had very close family members who said and *continue* to say very negative things.

When I made the decision to go to college I had one family member, one whom I actually looked up to, say to me, "Are you sure you want to go to college? What about community college? That is what your other relatives did." I felt angry at this comment from a family member, basically trying to kill my dreams and aspirations. Then when I decided to go to law school I had another *very* close family member say to me, "Are you sure that's what you want to do?" Can you imagine? Rather than words of encouragement, like "Great idea!" "You are going to make a great lawyer!" or "I will support you all they way," I got "are you sure?" I don't think either relative was trying to be malicious, but they both have been infected with excuse-tosis and were subconsciously spreading the disease.

I am still close with these family members, but there are other more explosive and more critical things that many other people are subjected to from their family members that are considered verbal abuse! *You* need to step back from your family to decide who in your family circle is holding you back. These are the people who need to take a leave of absence from your life. This can be done without hurting anyone's feelings—you just do it. The two family members I just mentioned probably have no idea that they made these comments and most certainly have no idea that I have distanced myself from them.

ASK FOR MORE EDUCATION—TAKE A CLASS

I have had the great fortune of having gone to college and then law school, and I've learned a lot of things. But the most interesting thing about education, and most of the curricula in the higher educational systems in the world, is that there are not classes on how to build confidence or how to become successful. Though I graduated confidently from law school, law school did not teach me how to become a lawyer, let alone how to be successful.

Most of the lessons I learned about success were achieved through life experience. Despite this, after my formal education I took a few classes about negotiation, and I also went through extensive sales training. It bothers me that the world's educational systems do not spend time on teaching success principles and techniques. If we as a human race were taught these skills at a young age, it is my belief that most of the world's problems, from poverty to genocidal violence, would not occur. Learning the success principles and techniques that are in this book and available to everyone in courses and seminars all over the world teaches us how to better interact and achieve greatness through strong morals, ethics, and values. We can then leave behind the negative activities of jealousy and hatred for others.

Check out your local university or community college and enroll yourself in classes on confidence. These are usually offered at night and are inexpensive. On my website, AskMore-GetMore.com, I also have a list of other classes that are offered around the world and also classes that can be completed online to help improve your chances of success.

FAILURE IS A DISEASE THAT CAN BE CURED

There is really no such thing as failure, unless you believe you have failed. Failure is temporary—unless you give up and allow it to become permanent. In fact, temporary failures, also known as "temporary defeats," make us stronger and prepare us for the future. I view each "temporary defeat" as a learning experience. I've said this before, and you need to say it every day: *I have never failed at anything; I have only experienced defeat, and I will learn from it.* This is one of the easiest things to understand; we never fail, rather we experience adversity, which truly makes us stronger. Failure is fatal and it ends the experience. By using your imagination, every negative experience or "failure" can truly be turned into a positive lesson.

At fourteen, I was arrested for driving around on a dirt bike like a crazy kid, and I sat in jail for several hours until my mother finally picked me up. I was embarrassed and apologetic, but that did not persuade the judge—he gave me one year on supervised probation! I thank God for that judge. I had to visit a probation officer every week, and I showed up for every meeting. When I was in the juvenile system, I decided to learn from this experience and take advantage of the resources given to me. My probation officer was a scary guy who commanded respect and demanded that I change my ways. Interestingly, he had played professional football in Canada, so we had a common interest. Too many kids who get in trouble simply take their punishment and don't learn from the experience or discover the "silver lining" of opportunity. I decided to improve my grades, discipline my time, and observe my surroundings.

Fast-forward to 2003. During my last semester of law school, I called the same district attorney who crucified me when I was in high school and asked him to hire me as an intern. He was delighted to hear from me and jumped at the chance to make right what he had done to a young kid. I became 303 Certified with the Supreme Judicial Court of the Commonwealth of Massachusetts as a district attorney, which means I could do everything a lawyer does under the supervision of a licensed attorney. Guess who I saw on a daily basis? My old probation officer! In fact we worked together on a couple of issues. The experience of being arrested when I was fourteen, which was negative and unfortunate, ultimately became a positive, life-changing experience. I became very interested in the law and observed how things worked within the judicial system. What seemed like a failure or act of deviance by a young kid turned into a positive experience that changed my life.

SILVER LINING

Some would say I have lived a tough life. I grew up poor, surrounded by drugs, and witnessing violence. I had very few role models, missed passing the bar exam the first time around, declared bankruptcy, and had to testify in a murder trial at a very young age.

These were all pretty hard things to go through. We all have personal struggles and tragedies. I taught myself that no matter how bad a situation is, I should always try to learn from it and search for the "silver lining" in the clouds. Adversity and challenges will always be present in your life, but once you are able to find the silver lining, things won't seem so bad. There is *always* a silver lining; you just need to train yourself to find it. One big silver lining for me is that today I realize the difficult times and struggles in my life have made me who I am and allowed me to write *Ask More, Get More* in order to change people's lives.

The reason I tell you the stories about my life is to show you that once you decide to make a change—at *any* age and from *any* background—it can be done. There is no stronger force than that of the human spirit. And believe me, there are many more amazing stories of overcoming adversity than mine.

But ultimately *Ask More, Get More* isn't about my or others' stories, it is about yours. It's about your commitment to change what you want to change right now. In my next book I want to tell your story. So start writing it *now*!

CHAPTER 2
ASK YOURSELF TO STOP MAKING EXCUSES

When you correct your mind, everything else will fall into place.

—Dr. Wayne Dyer

HOW I STOPPED MAKING EXCUSES AND STARTED MAKING MONEY

It wasn't until I was in my late twenties that I really understood how harmful excuses can become to a person's life, and I became consciously aware of "excusetosis." But even earlier, now that I look back, I realize that I was finding ways to overcome this awful disease from the time I was a child. When I discussed how I am no different than anyone else, that is true, but at a very young age I just learned not to make excuses. I learned how to shield myself from excusetosis through the advice of my mom and my teachers, but those who really drove home the harmful nature of excusetosis were my coaches. As I stated earlier, I played baseball, football, soccer, and even basketball when I was a child. My coaches were all working dads who decided to help out within the community by coaching. Looking back on it, I realize that coaching is such an awesome responsibility; as you are about to learn, the values they teach you will change your life—even when it's about something as simple as learning to bunt.

I think a lot of kids are afraid of getting hit by a baseball, and so the skill of bunting is somewhat intimidating. When you bunt a baseball, you essentially square your body over the plate and try to do what some would say is the hardest thing to do in all sports: make contact between a round bat and a round ball. I remember one day telling my coach that I just couldn't do it. My main excuse was that I was afraid of being hit by the ball. He said that every time I went up to the plate, that was a possibility. But I went on to explain very methodically that squaring the body over the plate would actually increase the chances of getting hit, and it could really hurt. He then explained to me the importance of the bunting technique and how it could cause a team to win or lose, so everyone had to learn how to bunt. I continued to say why I couldn't, and, somewhat exasperated, he had our star pitcher and me go up to the mound and throw balls at him as fast as possible, and he bunted every single one. I remember being amazed at his skill, but it still did not comfort me. Well, I finally tried it, and after a while I got the hang of it. Now, I was always a big kid, and when I got up to the plate, it was usually a home run or a strikeout (I wasn't the best batter).

The following Saturday we had a game on a baseball field that I am looking at as I type. The game wasn't one of any importance other than that we of course wanted to win. Well, as you can imagine, it was late in the game, bottom of the ninth, two outs, tied up 2–2 with a man on third and *guess who* was up to bat? Now, again, I was very inconsistent with my batting skills, so I looked over at my coach and he gave the signal for a bunt! A suicide squeeze is what it was actually called; I had to bunt the ball just so that it would go down the first base line, run as fast as I could, and my teammate would run from third and hopefully score and we would then be ahead by a run. Well, I had two options: not listen to my coach, swing for the bleachers, hit a home run, and gloriously walk off the field; or listen to what I was taught and bunt. Well, I decided not to make an excuse in my head as to why I would not listen to him, and I laid down the perfect bunt, right down the first base line. My teammate safely made it to home plate, and we won the game. I could have totally missed the ball, gotten hit, or not laid down the bunt properly, but I would never know the answer if I had made an excuse as to why I would not bunt the ball.

That day I learned a few lessons that don't need a lot of explanation. Number one: when you are being taught something by someone who knows more than you, listen. This person *knows more than you!* Number two: apply the skills you learned from your "coach" to whatever situation applies. Number three: making excuses takes away your opportunity to see what could have been. Don't ever be that person who says "If I had *only* listened to my coach; if I had only done this or that." Excuses can kill your dreams and goals, no matter how big or small.

EXCUSOLOGY: THE STUDY OF THE DISEASE OF EXCUSETOSIS (HOW TO REMOVE EXCUSES FROM YOUR MIND)

Many books discuss how excuses set us back and prevent us from achieving our goals. We all make and use excuses every day: I didn't work out today because I'm too busy, too tired, or there is not enough time in the day . . . I didn't accomplish my *goal* today because I was distracted by one of my colleagues . . . I wasn't able to give that presentation because I was afraid of what people would think of me . . . and on it goes. I could fill this entire chapter by listing thousands of excuses for every possible situation. Most of our excuses are just ways of making ourselves feel better about why we didn't do something, and oftentimes our loved ones help perpetuate this disease.

Your mom might have said to you when you were a kid, "That's okay, you didn't have enough time to practice, that's why you didn't make the team"; or "You're overweight because it's in our genes, you're big boned"; or "It's not your fault we are poor, it is the economy." Your parents were just trying to ease the pain of excusetosis by giving you more excuses, but in all reality they were acting as a secondary host of this disease and making you sicker.

When you study this disease you will find one very profound thing: successful people are either naturally immune or have developed an immunity to excusetosis. People who seem to have been born with an immunity to this disease most likely inherited this protective trait through their upbringing. Their parents didn't allow for excuses. Their teachers, coaches, and family members understood that exposure to this disease early on could have severe consequences in the attainment of success, and thus trained the child to develop the immunity to excusetosis. In all reality there are very few people brought up in this world who were never exposed to excusetosis, as most were infected at a very early age. It is airborne—it surrounds us via the television, radio, Internet, and in society as a whole. The good news is that excusetosis is curable at any stage in life, and curing it can have a profoundly positive impact on your life. The second you realize that this disease can only survive if the host allows it to live, you will be on your way to a more fulfilled life.

Before we go any further, I want you to think about something. Imagine for a moment that when a child begins to be able to walk he just decides that it is too hard because "I am too small," "It's not safe for me to walk," "I could bang my head," "I banged my knee, so I'm just going to crawl," "I can still get to where I need to go; it may take me a bit more time, but I will get there and most likely won't get hurt." Imagine what society would be like if that happened. *It would be a mess!* But, I also want you to understand that *everyone*, and this also includes children who are born with physical challenges, *everyone* is *not* born with excusetosis. In fact, our DNA does not have anywhere in it a gene that gives up. There is *not* an excuse gene. Excusetosis is a disease that is contracted from other human beings that can be transmitted many different ways. *You* were not supposed to make excuses, but somewhere along the way, you decided that it was okay to make them. Well, I'm sure you can tell by now, it is *not* okay to make excuses for setbacks in your life—*ever*!

SCHOOL LUNCH: ARE YOU BEING SERVED WHAT YOU WANT?

Ever since I can remember, my school meals were subsidized: at elementary school, middle school, and even high school. I remember being segregated from the other kids into a different line to get my food. It was humiliating. That feeling of being the poor kid or the kid whose parents couldn't provide was devastating for my psyche. I remember looking at the free-lunch kids and feeling like I didn't belong there. Even then I realized I wanted more out of life.

Before I continue, let me say there is nothing wrong with being in the free lunch line, and we are not lesser human beings because of it. But, I felt that way. There were many days where I would save money just so I could go in the "normal" line. I remember vividly going to the cashier and having to have her look up my name and check to make sure I was on the free lunch list—which simply added an exclamation point to the announcement to the world that I was a poor kid.

Many of the kids in that line felt the same way I did, but they also believed that they *were* lesser human beings and there was nothing that they could do about it. It is a horrible thing to realize, but most of them were fatally infected with excusetosis, and being separated from the other kids just allowed the disease to metastasize.

So when I am asked when that point in my life occurred when I truly stopped making excuses, I can point to bunting in baseball as the moment when I started to understand. But as for the point when I was consciously and deliberately curing myself of excusetosis, it really was in that school lunch line when the desire to be seen as more than just the poor kid was engrained into my brain. At that very young age I knew I wanted more. I remember telling my Aunt Lucia that I was going to be a millionaire by the time I was twenty-one. I didn't really know what that meant or how I would get there, but I knew I just didn't want to be poor anymore. I never really have had a desire to obtain material things that display success, but I just decided that I was going to get more out of life: more than what society thought I was worth, more than what my friends thought I was worth, and more than what my family believed I should be worth.

So for me, the cure for excusetosis was the desire to escape the stigma and reality of poverty and realizing that excuses would only hold me back. I didn't become a millionaire until about thirty-four, but I will never be that poor kid again. And it started at that point as a child when I said, "I am not going to make any excuses for being poor; I am simply not going to be poor!"

NO ARMS, NO LEGS

A while back I was watching ESPN and I saw a remarkable story that affirms my belief that we are *not* born with excusetosis. The story was about a man named Craig Dietz who was born in the rural town of St. Mary, Pennsylvania—without any arms or legs. Despite being born without limbs, Craig was a very active child, engaging in everything from bowling to hunting, and he was also an excellent student.

In addition to all of Craig's other sports-related activities, he had a passion for swimming, which seems impossible to most. After all, he has *no* arms and *no* legs! Craig actively competes in swim meets and even triathlons. Craig is also a lawyer and passed the bar exam the first time (good for him; it took me two tries!) without any accommodations from the Board of Bar Overseers. There are many other people just like Craig who prove my theory. You are not born with excusetosis, and you are not supposed to give up.

Now, when I discuss this disease with people, I get comments like, "What if they were born poor?" or "What if they were born disabled?" Some ask, "What if they suffered some sort of tragic event that prevented them from achieving their goals and dreams?" Tell that to Craig Dietz!

These statements are, in and of themselves, excuses. We can't determine when and where we are born, nor can we control freak accidents, but we can control our minds. Setbacks, temporary defeats, or physical limitations are not things that should call for an excuse. When toddlers fall down, they don't throw in the towel. They use that fall as a learning experience to achieve the goal of walking. Some children take longer than others, but all able-bodied children walk at some point.

OVERACTIVE KID TO OLYMPIAN

There is a story about a now-twenty-something guy who was a troublemaker, was very rambunctious, had concentration challenges, and was just a handful. Well, his mother got him involved in a team and also individual sports. He practiced every day to the point of exhaustion. He was very lucky to have amazing coaches who anticipated things such as the lights potentially going off during his competitions, and he even trained for that. That person is the most decorated Olympian in the United States, Michael Phelps.

His commitment to swimming, his discipline, and his ability to overcome adversity have made him one of the best athletes in the world, in any sport. One of the most remarkable stories about Michael Phelps was in the gold medal match in Beijing in 2008. The second he hit the water his goggles filled with water, and he swam the entire race unable to see! He not only won the gold but set the world record! Michael and his coaches prepared for what could go wrong by asking, "What if this happens? What will I do?" Michael chose to push through, not using any excuses, and relied on what he was taught. It is an amazing story. And it can be your story, too!

TO SLEEP OR NOT TO SLEEP

My senior year in high school, I was coasting through. I didn't have a solid plan as far as college, but I was pretty sure I was going to further my education. What I didn't realize at the time was that my senior year was extremely important with respect to my overall grade point average. I had gone from failing classes my freshman year to getting on the dean's list my senior year. But like many high school kids, especially seniors, I grew a little lazy and thought I could just coast through the rest of the year. Early on in the year I was tardy a lot, just missing classes due to pure laziness. I was oversleeping too much.

One fateful day when I was home in bed I got a phone call from my English teacher, and she told me that if I didn't show up, she would fail me and she would kick me out of her class! The nerve! About fifteen minutes later the head coach of the football team told me if I didn't show up he would kick me off the team. Let me put this in perspective: I was class president *and* captain of the football team. I felt that I was untouchable. "You can't fail me and kick me off the team," I thought. "Or can you?"

Well, one thing that I always respected was authority. I got my lazy ass out of bed and made it to English class and football practice. The incident could have changed my life for the worse if I came down with a case of excusetosis! Imagine what my life would look like now if I was kicked off the team and flunked English my senior year. The problem is, far too many people don't recognize moments in their life that are like the proverbial fork in the road. Pick one way and your life looks like this, pick the other and it looks like that. When I received two phone calls at 8:00 in the morning I was fortunately able to *ask* myself, "What would my life look like if I was kicked off the team and flunked English?" Doesn't take Nostradamus to answer that question. My coach and my English teacher helped to change my life that day, for the better. Thank you, Mr. Rosinski and Mrs. Nicholson! But, I also changed my own life by *asking* myself what would most likely happen if I did not show up. I respected not only authority but myself. I asked for more from myself!

SO WHAT'S YOUR EXCUSE?

As I have already shared, when I was a kid my surroundings were filled with despair, violence, drug abuse, and poverty. I could have used any of these as my excuse not to ask for more. But thankfully, when I was a kid and I asked my mother why life was always so hard, she responded with motherly love, "Things will get easier. Keep working. You will get through it." She never said, "It's hard because we are poor and have no money." When I was upset with a grade I received, she never said that I just wasn't smart enough. She said, "Keep trying and put your mind to it. You can do it."

When I graduated college in 1997, people told me I would not make more than $20,000 a year and not to expect more than that. This was despite the fact that I had decent grades, had interned for a congressman, and was class president for three years. Twenty thousand dollars? Really? I must admit that statement infected me for a while, and that's all I thought I was worth. But I quickly reprogrammed my mind and made double that my first year in the workforce!

Have you made an excuse for not getting something that you always wanted? Sure, we all have. But in order to actually achieve your goal, you need to cure the disease. There isn't a magic pill. No one else can do it but you. Opportunities are not going to slap you in the face. You will not wake up one day with everything you ever wanted—until you cure the disease of excusetosis.

So what now? What do you do to cure the disease? The good news is treatment can start today. Excusetosis is curable! You don't need insurance, you don't need a prescription, and you don't need money. You only need yourself and the willingness to cure yourself of this disease. Some symptoms are worse than others, but regardless of how severe a case of excusetosis you have, it can be cured.

STEP 1

The first thing you need to do is take total and full responsibility for where you are in life and be accountable for your past actions and all of your future decisions.

It is not your parents, your coworkers, your spouse, your boss, or anyone else's fault that you have this disease. We can't change what has happened to you, and you have to accept that fact. Looking back at what happened, how it happened, or why it happened will not cure the disease. You have to just accept that you are infected.

STEP 2

You need to accept that like many other diseases, excusetosis may come back. But if you are aware of the symptoms you can destroy it the same way chemotherapy kills cancer cells. The symptoms are not complex: any time you decide to blame something, someone, or some circumstance as to why a goal is not achieved, you will know the disease is back. At that point, step back, take a deep breath, and reprogram your mind. When you get into the *habit* of doing this day in and day out, at some point your habit will no longer be a habit but a natural subconscious action that will magically work for you. You control your thoughts, they do not control you.

HABIT: something you do every day so that it is involuntary and positive.

The best way to reprogram yourself—besides reading my book— is to remind yourself of all those people out there who could have made excuses but didn't, and how they changed the world. Then look at some of those people who aren't living up to their potential because they are making excuses.

MY DAD'S POTENTIAL EXCUSE

My dad is a perfect example. He is sixty-one years old (soon to be sixty-two). He is a hard worker and always has been, and he instilled the value of hard work in me when I was a kid. He used to take me out on weekends, but many times he had to work. At that time he was a "tree guy"—in other words, he cut down and removed trees. He took me with him and put me to work. I loved it. I hung out with my dad, learned what he did, and got paid! Most recently he was working as a machinist, and he was concerned about his current job because of his age. He was worried that if he was laid off or lost his job, it would be very difficult to get another job because he is "too old." Later on in the book I tell the story about how I taught my dad some simple techniques that not only cured his excusetosis, but also increased his personal net worth.

HENRY FORD'S POTENTIAL EXCUSE

Henry Ford didn't start Ford Motor Company until he was forty-five, well after his peak earning potential. Would Ford Motor Company have ever been created if Henry Ford thought he was "too old"? Henry Ford may have been halfway through his life when he started Ford Motor Company, but his life experience and temporary defeats prepared him for founding one of the most successful companies in existence today. Henry Ford didn't think he was too old to start a gigantic, multinational company. He knew his age was an asset.

THEO EPSTEIN'S POTENTIAL EXCUSE

One of the classic excuses in life, and the inverse of "I'm too old," is "I'm too young." Ageitis, a form of excusetosis, is also curable. Theo

Epstein was twenty-eight when he became the general manager of one of baseball's most iconic teams, the Boston Red Sox. Theo was certainly too young to be the general manager of a baseball team in one of the most unforgiving markets in the country, a team that has a current value of close to $700 million—right? Many people thought that, but in 2004, under Theo Epstein, the Red Sox won their first World Series in eighty-six years, and then did it again in 2007. Imagine what the team would be like if Theo thought he was "too young." Rather than thinking Theo was too young and inexperienced, the ownership saw a smart kid who had drive, who worked while he was in law school, who studied baseball, and who dreamed about working for the Boston Red Sox. Theo's age was never an issue for him or the ownership of the Red Sox. I have managers working for me who are in their twenties, and they manage teams of people who are of all ages—most of them much older than my managers. They are my managers because they are good at what they do—period!

MICHAEL ALDEN'S POTENTIAL EXCUSE (JUST ONE OF MANY I HAD TO CHOOSE FROM)

I'm not smart enough! I could have easily chosen to believe that. But it is not the amount of education or the prestige of your educational source; rather it is what you get out of it.

You know how many times I heard that I wasn't smart enough? When I was a senior in high school, my guidance counselor tried to inject me with a lethal dose of excusetosis by telling me, "College isn't for everyone." I will never forget that day. This guy was my guidance counselor, a person who was supposed to help me succeed! Several years later I was in the ICU unit at the hospital where my grandmother was dying, and amazingly it just so happened that my guidance counselor was in the room adjacent to my grandmother's, visiting a sick relative of his own. I said hello to him and just thanked him. I could have said something nasty to my guidance counselor, and I admit, I wanted to; but as you will learn, negative behavior would have been counterproductive and would not accomplish anything, not to mention that we were both saying goodbye to loved ones. Instead, I thanked my guidance counselor, because his lack in belief in me essentially drove me to prove him wrong. I'm sure that every day we all face doubts from others about our abilities. Ask yourself, "What will I do to prove them wrong?"

Intelligence has *nothing* to do with success. What is intelligence, anyway? Well, this book isn't the book to expound on what is smart or whether or not you are intelligent. If you have this book in your hands, you can answer both questions in the affirmative. *You* are smart and intelligent. Why? Because you decided to change your future. You are smart and intelligent at *everything* you do. Believe it! Repeat this phrase and write it down in the margin of this book or somewhere that will ensure you will see it every day, then do it every day until you have programmed your subconscious mind to believe it. Throughout my book I reference several other books. Get copies of these books; they are like vitamins for your brain that help suppress the disease of excusetosis.

NOT MY FAULT: MY BROTHER'S EXCUSE

I was at my brother's wedding a few months back, and I was sitting next to one of my other brothers. I love all of my family members, so this is a tough thing to write about. He spent most of his life in and out of prison, is addicted to drugs, and has overdosed several times. One time when he overdosed he actually died and had to be revived. But, like people say, the truth hurts. I asked my brother how he was, and of course he said he was doing well, but anyone could clearly tell that he wasn't okay. I asked him about his goals and more specifically where he was on his apprenticeship as an electrician. He told me, "Dad screwed it up."

So I inquired, "What happened? How did Dad screw up your career goals?"

He proceeded to tell me that while he was in prison, Dad didn't pay the renewal fee for his license. He was adamant! My brother was in prison . . . and Dad screwed it up? I looked my brother in the eye and said, "You screwed it up," and he retorted, "How did I screw it up? I was *locked up*." I smiled and said, "Exactly! You were *locked up*, and that's why you screwed it up."

Now, I'm pretty sure I didn't get through to him, and I am saddened to tell you that he went on to overdose again—a fourth time—and this time he passed away. But as terrible as that is, it is *never* anyone else's fault. Once you realize that and accept it, you will find that your path to success and happiness will be smooth.

NOT OUR FAULT!

Sometimes I wonder when bad things happen at my company, when there are technical errors, or when things just don't go right, if maybe it really isn't our fault. There have been times when it seems like there was a common force continually working against us. Is it really not our fault? For example, when our phone system shuts down, or when an advertisement doesn't air when it is supposed to, or when we lose electricity in our building, or when packages get lost in the mail—the obvious fault of third parties, right? These are things that are outside of our control . . . right? Wrong!

ACCOUNTABILITY: our ability to acknowledge our own acts and take responsibility for those acts.

We can't control everything, but we can prepare for things to go wrong and have systems in place so that when others interfere with our success, it won't matter. I tell my executives, it is *never* the phone company's fault, the electric company's fault, the postal service's fault. It is our fault: everyone at my company is *accountable*, and it is *never* a third party's fault. Be accountable, and you will be successful in anything that you do.

THE TIME ISN'T RIGHT

Well, when is the time ever right? The light is *never* going to be green. The stars will *never* be perfectly aligned. Why is it that people always wait till the first of the year to make their resolution? That is an excuse. I know a guy who is a smoker and has been for fifteen years. One day in January he posted on one of the major social networking sites that he was quitting smoking in August because that was the month his daughter was born, and she deserved better. I guess she didn't deserve better for the seven months in between. He continues to this day to post that he is changing his habits but never does. I recently reached out to him and told him that he needs to *do it*. Stop telling people you are going to change; just *do it*! Why wait? Every day you smoke it decreases the amount of time you will be on this planet and the time you will spend with your daughter.

Why is it that all diets start on Monday? Why wait? You know what happens the weekend before? People gorge themselves and then attempt to diet.

If you want to do something, don't wait for the timing to be right. I recently bought some silver, and a friend of mine told me how it is going to drop in price and that I should wait. Well, he may be right, and it may be a mistake, and if so I will learn from it, but how would I feel if the current price of silver skyrockets to $180 an ounce? The time was right for me. I could make excuses for the next ten years to justify why *not* to buy, and I could convince myself not to buy if I listened to others.

STEP 3

The third thing you need to do *every* time you find yourself making an excuse is instantly find a reason why it can be done. That way, it will get done. You may find that along the way you will be faced with dozens, if not hundreds, of excuses for why you can't. All you have to do is tell yourself it can and *will* be done. Does this seem too simple? Some may think so, but you have this book in your hands, and you spent your hard-earned money to purchase it. Don't spread the disease by making excuses as to why you can't do something.

YOU CAN AND YOU WILL!

Here are just a few of the common excuses that begin to infect us, along with some provided phrases to immunize you against this disease. Every time you hear yourself saying one of the tired phrases on the left, change it to the inspired phrase on the right.

You have your own symptoms that you need to diagnose and cure. Curing yourself starts *today*. It may take a little time, but once you are cured, this book and everything else in your life will become more fulfilling than you ever imagined.

I can't make it work	**I WILL MAKE IT WORK**
It is too difficult	**IT'S CHALLENGING, BUT I WILL GET IT**
I'm not good enough	**I WILL GET BETTER**
I'm too out of shape	**I'M GOING TO GET HEALTHY**
I can't do that	**I WILL DO THAT**

I will do it later	**I WILL DO IT NOW**
I can't finish in time	**I WILL FIND THE TIME**
It's risky	**I WILL FIND A WAY TO MAKE IT WORK**
I don't deserve it	**I DO DESERVE IT**
I can't afford it	**I WILL FIND THE MONEY TO GET WHAT I WANT**
It's not my fault	**I ACCEPT RESPONSIBILITY, AND I WILL RECTIFY IT**
It's never happened before	**IT WILL HAPPEN**
I can't	**I CAN**
Not possible	**IT IS POSSIBLE**
I'm tired	**I'M ALIVE, AWAKE, AND READY FOR THE DAY/TASK AT HAND**

THE MERCHANT PROCESSOR: THE ULTIMATE EXCUSE I DIDN'T MAKE

Imagine this: After about one year of bootstrapping my business, millions of dollars in debt and one foot over the brink of failure, I made the decision to expand our offices and the business. Most of my executives were nervous and not sure about the decision. I knew that it was what we needed in order to survive. So, I borrowed more money and had our offices custom built to suit our needs.

Now imagine this: About a week after moving into our new offices I received a FedEx from my merchant processor (the company that allows me to process credit cards) that said they had seized almost $300,000 and that they were terminating my ability to process credit cards. At the time, processing credit cards was my business's primary and only way to receive funds and sell things. We had almost two hundred employees, growing debt, and no way to process credit cards. *And* they had seized almost $300,000! Oh, and did I mention . . . it was a payroll week?

The story is pretty involved, but ultimately it boils down to the fact that this company had it in for me and was trying to slice my throat and put me out of business. In fact, they actually told me that they were going to put me out of business. I was in complete shock! The good news was that I had a backup merchant processor, and I was able to move my business to them. The bad news is that the amount of business we moved made my new processor very nervous and they, too, were telling me they were going to shut me off!

If those events had caused me to go out of business, it would have been very easy to blame my demise on others. But I would not allow myself to even entertain what would have been a totally understandable excuse. My family, my employees, and their families relied on my ability to keep our business afloat in order to put food on their tables. An excuse just was not an option. So I met with several other processors who were extremely reluctant to even speak with me due to the fact that I had been terminated and that I was involved in a lawsuit with my previous processor. But I persevered and refused to take no for an answer. Ultimately, I was able to secure a new processor to whom I am forever grateful. They knew we were good people running a good business. As I type, I have systems in place to make sure that what happened to us will never happen again. At our company we do not blame third parties for mistakes or adversity. Instead, we try to have the foresight to look into the future and anticipate what could happen or what could go wrong.

Some would say that is a negative way to think; they are wrong. Looking ahead and trying to anticipate what could go wrong is actually the responsible and rational thing to do. I am a hack chess player, but in chess you are always trying to think about your next move. The best chess players in the world know not only their next move, but they can anticipate what their opponent will do and they know what they will do in order to win. Ask yourself, what is your next move? What does the future look like? Can you do something now to anticipate a future event so that it will ensure your success? The answer is *yes*, you can and you should.

EDUCATE YOURSELF

One other great way to cure excusetosis is through personal education. Throughout the book I mention several other books that have had a positive impact on my life, and I suggest you read them. Go to your local library and search the personal development section. Download a free ebook. This does not have to cost you a dime.

Zig Ziglar once told me that he reads three hours a day—every day. He also tells a great story in his book about his secretary— who has her master's degree from what Ziglar calls "Automobile

University"—utilizing time spent in traffic to educate herself. She has no formal education, but listening to CDs to and from work every day helped her achieve success. Take it from the expert: educate yourself to cure yourself and improve your life.

CHAPTER 3
ASK YOURSELF TO SHAPE UP YOUR BODY

GROW YOUR BANK ACCOUNT, NOT YOUR GUT!

Why do I dedicate an entire chapter in my book to the topics of health and wellness? Because your physical health affects your mental health. When your body isn't healthy, your mind is almost always unhealthy as well. And you cannot ask for *more* from your life if you are not asking for *more* from your own body and your own mind. If you do *ask* more out of your body, it will definitely bring you *more*.

Was I always in shape? Well, that is a complex question to answer. When I was a kid my mom used to buy my clothes at Ann & Hope in the Husky section. It was a nice way of saying "the fat kid section." We also bought my clothes in the irregular section, because my body wasn't "regular." What the hell does "irregular" mean? I don't know, but it wasn't a positive thing.

Now, I don't think I was really a "fat" kid, or "irregular." But I was always big, and I do remember how it made me feel. I felt like a "fat irregular" kid. I may have developed a body image complex as a result, but the positive side of what really happened was that I became very interested in sports, health, and nutrition. I didn't become fanatical about how I ate or about my body, but I became acutely aware of how nutrition and exercise affected my body. And that wasn't always easy, because when you are a poor kid, nutrition is not as important as having a full belly. And I wasn't always able to get healthy things to eat, because even back then, healthy food was expensive. But I digress.

RATS! NOT ALL THAT TALK ABOUT NUTRITION AGAIN!

To make a long story interesting, I think the way I came to ask for *more* out of my nutrition was thanks to rats. In ninth grade biology class we had to do a science project that not only had to be presented to the class, but was also automatically entered in the school science fair. Around this same time I was becoming increasingly involved in working out. I started to read magazines such as *Flex* and *Muscle and Fitness* and was very interested in supplementation. I discovered ginseng and how it had an energizing effect. I began taking ginseng before workouts and even before practices and noticed a significant increase in energy. So, I decided that my science fair project would be "The Effect of Ginseng on Rats." Now this was twenty-plus years ago, and ginseng wasn't in every food product and health and beauty product as it is now. I conducted a six-week study on how ginseng affected the behavior in rats. I had a control group and an experimental group. Every day I gave the experimental group ginseng, while the control group did not receive ginseng. My results validated my own personal experimentation with ginseng: the experimental group was much more active, they actually grew faster, and they seemed to be more energetic during their time on the wheel versus the control group.

Now as you already know, I was a kid who at this time was not the best academically. But after presenting my "super rats" to my class, I received an A on the project and I got to spend a Saturday at the science fair presenting my project to scientists and other judges. At the time I thought it was a waste of time. But during the fair I noticed that I had more interest in my booth than others in the science fair. At the end of the day, when awards were being presented and we were breaking down our displays, I was called to the stage! I actually took second place in the science fair! Most of my fellow students were in complete shock and were making excuses as to why they didn't win—even accusing me of somehow making the entire project up. Well, I knew that I had put the work in, and I was extremely proud of my project. I remember what it was like receiving the award in front of my peers; it felt very good. That moment in the ninth grade obviously inspired an interest in nutrition, but it also changed the way I thought about my grades. There is a diametrical difference between receiving an A and an F, and the emotional gratification of an A is euphoric. I not only began to think more about health and nutrition but also about how good it felt getting the acclaim and reward of good grades for my hard work.

IF IT WEREN'T FOR ATHLETICS . . . I WOULD NOT BE THE PERSON I AM TODAY

Athletics, and particularly team sports, changed the way my body looked, but more importantly they shaped my mind. Team sports directly and indirectly teach discipline, humility, respect, how to deal with adversity, time management, how to interact with others, how to win, how to lose, and how to work as a team. Entire books and courses in colleges all across the country are teaching future coaches how to teach their players these skills. I was very fortunate to have parents who got me involved in sports at a very young age. In my first experience of soccer we were the champions of our league at about the age of eight. My team name was the Sharks and the trophies we received were bigger than us! And then my first experience in football was even better—yes, better! We were undefeated and unscored-on champions! I was about ten, and it was Peewee football. I played guard and center. The field was only eighty yards, but still, no other team scored on us for the entire season!

This was where I had a chance to turn an excuse into an asset. When it came to football, I was lucky to be the "husky" kid, and because of my size I dominated at a very young age. In the book *Outliers*, Malcolm Gladwell discusses how athletes who excel get more attention from coaches and thus get better as a result. It is true, and I know it is, because I was treated a little differently on the football field. I wasn't the poor kid in the free lunch line anymore; I was a dominating force on the field. Still, I was never coddled. My coaches used to yell at me, push me, make me do laps, and expect more out of me. This type of attention I did not like. But it was teaching me how to be humble and respect my coaches even if I did not agree with their tactics.

As a result of my ability to respect my coaches, I began to respect the team and was very disciplined. There were many times throughout my life where my mom did not have a car, but that did not mean I could miss practice, so I used to put my football gear on and ride my bike to and from practice! There were several other kids in my neighborhood and other poor neighborhoods who did the same thing, but there were also kids who used the excuse of not being able to get to practice as a way to skip. Guess what happened to those kids? The coaches lost faith and did not pay attention to them.

This is just an example of what happens in life. If you withdraw from the Emotional Bank Account (I will discuss this more in the next chapter) in any aspect of your life, it is extremely difficult to even get back to a zero balance, let alone a surplus. I realized this at a very young age and made sure that not only did I make it to practice, but when I was there I worked hard.

The football program at Beverly High School was extremely competitive, and there were a lot of talented athletes. As a freshman, if you were good enough you were called up to practice with the varsity team to help them prepare for the Thanksgiving game. So, the reward for being good was . . . another two weeks of practice? Two weeks of getting knocked around by actual men, and two weeks of getting teased and hazed—this was the reward? Yes it was, because it was an *opportunity* for me to show the varsity coaches what they had to look forward to in me. For those two weeks in the bitter cold I got knocked down, pushed, punched, and even knocked out a few times.

There were a couple of freshmen, and we were essentially human dummies and sacrificial lambs. But our actual job was to make the team better. I went full-speed all the time and got beat up bad every day. One particular senior guard hated me! I was making him look bad, because I was getting through the line and really was just a better athlete. But he was *huge*! His name was Tom and he did not like me! On one play he literally grabbed my shoulder pads and punched me in the throat. All of this went unnoticed by the coaches, or maybe they were simply looking the other way. Now, obviously some of Tom's actions were straight-up dirty and nasty, but I was learning how to deal with adversity, learning how to know my place, and at the same time showing the coaches who I was. I was *exploiting* my *opportunity* to *be more*! That year we had a close Thanksgiving game, but we won. When I was on the bus in my clean and white uniform—because freshmen don't play in the Thanksgiving game— Tom came up to me and thanked me. He thanked me for pushing him and making him better. It was such a great feeling. At that moment I realized that my efforts, my ability to overcome physical adversity, my ability to respect authority, and my ability to work with a team played a small part in the win that day.

A HEALTHY BODY EQUALS A HEALTHY MIND— AND A HEALTHY WALLET

So in everything from rats to rushing the quarterback on the field, I had the opportunity to learn the importance and value of physical health and fitness when I was young, and it changed my life in many ways. Years later I came to realize that many of the world's most successful people have the same respect for health and fitness. I had the opportunity to learn more of its impact on your life from none other than Zig Ziglar. In his book, *See You at the Top*, Zig discusses how he was overweight and sluggish and how he made the decision to lose a pound a day. Weight loss has obvious health benefits, but more importantly the change in your appearance improves your self-image and your confidence, two very important things we all need to be healthy.

While I dined with Mr. Ziglar at Legal Seafood, a restaurant known for serving large seafood portions, one of the guests ordered lobster. The server stated that they only had three-pound lobsters. This guest ordered the lobster, and it was so big that people walked over from other tables to take pictures of it. Mr. Ziglar ordered a baked potato, steamed broccoli, and grilled haddock. He went on to tell me that once he set the goal to lose the weight, he never gained it back. Zig acknowledges in his book that after losing thirty-seven pounds, his personal image improved. He also felt it was important to preach the values and attributes of improving your mental and physical health with equal importance.

Later I attended the "fifty-ninth anniversary" of Mr. Ziglar's twenty-first birthday, a grand event at the Gaylord Texan at which no alcohol could be found. Zig Ziglar is one of the best motivational speakers I have ever seen, and his books have been sold all over the world. Anything he does or doesn't do is definitely worth paying attention to, and I highly recommend his books as well.

Napoleon Hill, the author of *The Law of Success* and *Think and Grow Rich*, was a man of great importance in the field of positive thinking and success. Hill believed that in order to become successful, you have to cleanse your system. Cleansing is also another great technique that has been used for thousands of years all over the world to maintain youth. There are all types of bodily cleanses— liver, colon, kidney, lungs, lymphatic system, and others. The following is an excerpt from *The Law of Success*. This section is reprinted unedited, not as a guide or a recommendation for cleansing, but rather as a beginning of your understanding of how a healthy body equals a healthy mind. On just two pages of this book, there's enough sound advice to keep the average person healthy and ready for action during sixteen of the twenty-four hours of the day, but the advice is so simple that most people would not follow it.

AN EXCERPT FROM *THE LAW OF SUCCESS*

The amount of work that I perform every day and still keep in good physical condition is a source of wonderment and mystery to those who know me intimately. Yet there is no mystery to it, and the system I follow does not cost anything and here it is, for your use if you want it:

First: I drink a cup of hot water when I first get up in the morning, before I have breakfast.

Second: My breakfast consists of rolls made of whole wheat and bran, breakfast cereal, fruit, soft-boiled eggs once in a while, and coffee. For luncheon I eat vegetables (most any kind), whole wheat bread, and a glass of butter-milk. For supper, I usually enjoy a well-cooked steak once or twice a week, along with vegetables (especially lettuce) and coffee.

Third: I walk an average of ten miles a day: five miles into the country and five miles back, using this period for meditation and thought. When it comes to building health, perhaps the thinking is just as valuable, as a health builder, as the walk.

Fourth: I lie across a straight-bottom chair, flat on my back, with most of my weight resting on the small of my back, with my head and arms relaxed completely, until they almost touch the floor. These movements give the nervous energy of my body an opportunity to properly balance and distribute itself; ten minutes in this position will completely relieve all signs of fatigue, no matter how tired I may be.

Fifth: I take an enema at least once every ten days, and more often if I feel the need of it, using water that is a little below blood temperature, with a table-spoonful of salt in it, chest and knee position.

Sixth: I take a hot shower bath, followed immediately by a cold shower, every day, usually in the morning when I first get up.

These simple things I do for myself. Mother Nature tends to everything else necessary for my health.

I cannot lay too much stress upon the importance of keeping the intestines clean, for it is a well-known fact that the city dwellers of today are literally poisoning themselves to death by neglecting to cleanse their intestines with water.

You should not wait until you are constipated to take an enema. When you get to the stage of constipation, you are practically ill and immediate relief is absolutely essential, but if you will give yourself the proper attention regularly, just as you attend to keeping the outside of your body clean, you will never be bothered with constipation.

For more than fifteen years, no single week ever passed without my having a headache. Usually I administered a dose of aspirin and got temporary relief. I was suffering with auto-intoxication and did not know it, for the reason that I was not constipated.

When I found out what my trouble was I did two things, both of which I recommend to you. Namely, I quit using aspirin and I cut down my daily consumption of food nearly one-half.

Just a word about aspirin—a word which those who profit by its sale will not like—it effects no permanent cure of headache. Aspirin producers will not tell you about this, but it's true. What it does might be compared to a lineman that cuts the telegraph wire while the operator is using that wire in a call for aid; suppose that the operator is calling the fire department in order to save the burning building in which he is located. Aspirin cuts or "deadens" the line or nerve communication that runs from the stomach or the intestinal region, where auto-intoxication is pouring poison into the blood, allowing it to eventually reach into the brain, where the effect of that poison is registering its call in the form of intense pain.

Cutting the telegraph line over which a call for the fire department is being sent does not put out the fire; nor does it remove the root cause of your pain. The nerve line over which a headache is registering is simply a call for help.

You cannot be a person of action if you permit yourself to go without proper physical attention until auto-intoxication takes your brain and kneads it into an inoperative mass that resembles a ball of putty. Neither can you be a person of action if you eat the usual devitalized concoction called "white bread"—which has had all the real food value removed from it—and twice as much meat as your system can digest and properly dispose of.

You cannot be a person of action if you run to the pill bottle every time you have—or imagine you have—an ache or pain, or swallow an aspirin tablet every time your intestines call on your brain for a douche bag of water and a spoonful of salt for cleansing purposes.

You cannot be a person of action if you overeat and under-exercise.

You cannot be a person of action if you read the patent medicine booklets and begin to imagine yourself ailing with the symptoms described by the clever advertisement writer, who has reached your pocketbook through the power of suggestion.

Amazingly, the preceding excerpt is in a book about success, not about health or wellness. But Napoleon Hill understood that in order to truly be healthy, we need to rid our body of impurities. Cleansing the body is another well-known way to improve one's health; its benefits range from curing disease to improving energy and vitality. And ultimately we know that our physical health does impact our mental health.

THE JIM SHRINER STORY

Jim Shriner, the author of *Live Disease Free to 103*, is a very good friend of mine. Jim's story is nothing short of amazing. When he was sixteen he was diagnosed with a tumor in his vertebrae that caused paralysis. Through a long surgical procedure by a revolutionary doctor, the tumor was removed and his vertebrae rebuilt. At that time Jim made the decision to rebuild his body and his mind. He went on to become Mr. Indiana and was one of the original contestants on *American Gladiator*. Today Jim is fifty years old and in amazing shape. He lives an abundant life and is one of the most energetic and inspirational people I know. Jim told me that when he was in the hospital in a full body cast and not sure if he would ever walk again, he began to think about how his body was truly a temple. When he was finally able to get released from the hospital, he dedicated his life to not only his own body but also to helping others. He became a trainer and developed products for others, and he really has as his heart's desire helping others live disease-free. Jim's physical appearance is a reflection of his mental attitude.

He looks good and always feels good. He has more energy than anyone I have ever met. He recently told me that he is 186 pounds and ripped—at fifty! The interesting thing about Jim—and many others who experience a life-changing, traumatic event and overcome it—is that his mental attitude is always positive. You don't need a traumatic event to change your health, but many people wait until it's too late to get healthy. Move forward with your health, or you will be moving backward.

FIND THE SWAN IN YOU

Greg Comeaux was the original trainer in the hit TV show *The Swan*. Greg is almost sixty years of age, and he has less than 6 percent body fat. Greg has always been an athlete and in good shape, but what inspires me about Greg is that with age he seems to get in better shape. He is mentally sharp, a true physical specimen, and continues to help people all over the country maintain a healthy lifestyle. His effervescent personality is infectious, and he motivates me to continue to hit the gym, ride my bike, go for walks, and generally keep pushing. Just today I was in a crossfit class and I truly felt like I was going to vomit. But I remember working out with Greg years ago, and his personal drive pushed me through my workout. Greg has residences all over the United States but spends most of his time in Southern California, where everyone almost always seems to have "something going on." Greg, too, has many irons in the fire, and most never pan out. But he always pushes forward, and it is because at the age of almost sixty, he feels good physically and mentally, even when faced with constant disappointment. He is constantly writing, training, and speaking to others. To put it in perspective, I have produced probably a dozen infomercials with Greg for various products of his, from weight loss products to energy drinks that he endorses. Only one of them ever worked—and it paid off. That's why it pays to stay positive, despite setbacks; you're only one win away from success!

DON'T INDULGE!

Several years ago I was at my gym and I saw on the wall what looked like a project from a high school student. It was an advertisement for a book called *The Health Club Diet*. I loved the title and I asked one of my executives to find the author and *ask* him if he would be interested in having my company market his book. His name is Michael Atwood, and he is a humble, down-to-earth fitness trainer who created a blueprint for people to lose weight and stay fit. Now, I have seen everything that people have created to lose weight: from fitness machines to magical weight loss pills. But, what made Atwood's approach unique was his ability to recognize that most Americans are going to indulge. He taught in his book how to be less of a glutton. Since I met Atwood, my company has marketed his book and I have also had the good fortune to be trained by him. I don't know his age, but he is over forty and he lives and breathes his book. He also inspires me to keep exercising and getting better. What I like about Michael's book and Michael as a person is that he knows that being successful can truly be simple once you recognize that little changes will make a huge difference in your physical and mental health.

PHYSICAL ACTIVITY MEANS BRAIN ACTIVITY!

Physical activity releases chemicals like dopamine in our body and makes us feel good. When dopamine is released, neurotransmitters become activated and blood and oxygen flow more easily through our body. We cannot function without blood and oxygen. When the blood is flowing properly and your brain is receiving the proper amount of oxygen, you will think more clearly. When you are physically able to do things, you are able to *ask* more out of everything—from others and from yourself.

When I exercise, I increase my creativity and solve problems. As I discussed earlier, I am now almost addicted to yoga. I love the challenge and what it does for my body and mind. Find something you like to do that is physical, and do it every day. Your mind and your body will thank you for it.

POWER YOGA

As I have said in my advertisements for *Ask More, Get More*, anybody can apply the techniques and strategies in this book. Yoga is one of the techniques that, when applied, will enhance your life in ways you never imagined. Yoga is of course considered meditation, but power yoga contains more of a fitness approach, and there is an emphasis on maintaining strength, good posture, and flexibility. It is understood as a practice to maintain a healthy lifestyle—whether to reduce stress, for emotional healing, controlling heart conditions, or even enhancing memory and learning. Doctors and healthcare providers are becoming more open minded about yoga and recommending the practice to their clients and patients at an increasing rate.

Yoga incorporates a certain type of breathing: a deep, long, and slow inhalation from your nose that glides over the top of your throat. It almost sounds like ocean movement. The exhalation, out through your mouth, has the same sound and feel. The deep, repetitive, and very controlled breathing sets your sails for a peaceful and stress-free meditation.

During this meditation there is a boost in oxytocin, a hormone in the body that is associated with feeling relaxed and connected to others. Yoga also helps stabilize your mood, and the intense breathing in yoga boosts the levels of oxygen in your brain for added awareness. Yoga is also believed by some to help with depression and obsessive-compulsive disorder.

Increasing numbers of Americans are experiencing some type of heart disease due to a sedentary lifestyle. Those who practice yoga slow their heart rate down, which in turn lowers their blood pressure. This is a way to help prevent strokes and lower the risk of having to go through heart surgery. Power yoga is practiced in a heated room, so you are perspiring and sweating out the toxins that you have consumed. Yoga also may lower cholesterol and boost your immune system. The best part of yoga and meditating is that every individual can modify his or her movements to what feels good individually. Of course, there are some positions that need to be done in a certain way and may feel uncomfortable, but in total, power yoga relaxes and soothes your mind, body, and soul.

TAKE A WALK OUTSIDE

Getting outside is a great way to reset your mind. Spending time outside, no matter what the weather, naturally improves your health, and what's better than that? There's something soothing about being outside. One cannot deny that the fresh scents of nature calm your mind and body. On the other hand, there is no question that the stifling heat of summer or frigid cold of winter can make attempts at outdoor activity less inviting. But becoming aware of all of the health benefits may give you that extra push to head outside to walk.

While on your walk, make sure you take in those big, deep breaths of fresh air. Fresh air supplies us with a strong flow of oxygen, which is extremely important for our brains. We all need fresh air, especially those who are sick or whose bodies are in a stage of healing or repairing. The best air to breathe in is typically around plants, trees, rivers, waterfalls, and oceans, especially right after a thunderstorm.

Here are just some of the benefits that you can naturally gain from being outside:

› helps the airways of your lungs dilate;

› improves the cleansing process of your lungs;

› helps improve your heart and blood pressure rates;

› helps your immune system fight off disease more effectively;

› stimulates your appetite and helps digest your food better;

› improves concentration by clearing your mind.

Many people go on their daily walks to keep up their physical health. However, changing up the scenery and taking a walk in a peaceful and natural setting can help reduce stress levels by giving individuals a sense of connectivity to themselves. The feeling of "escaping" is relaxing and also exciting, and it may help ease the pressures of the day. A more relaxed state of mind leads to various healthy achievements.

An easy, low-impact walk is all you need; it does not have to be vigorous by any means. The long, steady pace will help you ease into a higher level of conditional strength and overall health. Walking is the most inexpensive and simplest way to exercise. Start today. It does not take long. Start with a ten-minute walk, and you are on your way to a healthier you!

Some other benefits of walking:

› staying strong;

› feeling more energetic;

› helps you sleep better;

› improves self-esteem;

› weight management;

› lower levels of cholesterol;

› reduces risk of or helps manage type-2 diabetes;

› reduces risk of heart disease, stroke, high blood pressure, and colon cancer;

› protects against falling and bone fractures in older adults;

› helps control joint swelling and discomfort from arthritis.

I mention yoga and walking, because almost anybody can do these activities. There are different, less vigorous types of yoga for beginners, and more rigorous types of walking, but both forms of activity still have the same effect on the body and mind. If you are for some reason physically challenged, then try meditation. Meditation and visualization are great ways to keep your mind healthy. There are many other activities that we can all do to stay healthy; just choose one that works best for you. Whether it is weight training, walking, riding a bike, or gardening, physical activity improves your spirit, mind, and body.

THE BODY RESURRECTS THE MIND AND VICE VERSA

Several years ago a woman gave birth to an amazing little girl. This woman had always been in shape her whole life. She was a yoga instructor and lived in a part of the country where almost everyone was in shape. After her pregnancy she gained roughly fifty pounds and could not lose the weight. She was fatigued and beginning to feel depressed about her struggles. She was then diagnosed with lupus, a debilitating disease in which your immune system essentially attacks your own organs and joints. She has the kind that attacks her joints. When everything seemed almost hopeless, she decided that she was going to enter fitness competitions! At forty-one this woman—my wife, Kristin—went on to not only enter but win several fitness competitions and inspired other post-pregnancy moms to get in shape and stay fit. She did it by *asking* herself to commit to a very rigid diet and exercise plan. Well, she still has lupus, but she is in fantastic shape, and her pain due to the lupus has reduced dramatically. Her thought process was that of a contrarian. Most people in her situation would allow excusetosis to infect them and give them a reason to just give up. She did the complete opposite and *asked more* out of herself physically, and she was compensated tenfold, mentally and emotionally.

DRUGS CHANGED MY LIFE—DON'T LET THEM CHANGE YOURS FOR THE WORSE

When I was about ten, my dad admitted himself into a rehabilitation center for a cocaine addiction. My parents were divorced, so I didn't really notice anything, but my dad had the good sense to know he had a problem. About one week into his rehabilitation he asked that I come visit him. I vividly remember visiting him in a place that was like a hospital and him sitting me down to explain why he was there. Now at ten, I think it was difficult for me to understand, but I remember not wanting to be there again.

My stepfather died of AIDS contracted because of a heroin addiction. My mother was infected by him. My brother, my stepfather's son, was also in rehab for heroin. A cousin of mine is addicted to methamphetamines and is a lady of the evening. Another cousin was in a car accident that almost killed everyone in the car, and one passenger is in a persistent vegetative state. My cousin wrecked the car because he was high, and he served five years in prison. I have another family member who is addicted to prescription pills and, as a result, can't work. I have friends who have overdosed and died. Every single person I know started out smoking cigarettes, then smoking pot, and then moving on to the next drug.

Now, I am not judging anyone, and several people that I know, including some of the above, who have had substance abuse issues have recovered and are doing well. I drink socially, which is admittedly using a drug, but for me doing something illegal takes it to a whole new level. Certainly, alcohol can destroy one's life just like any other drug. But, for me, after seeing what illegal drugs do to people, I decided not to even experiment. Nothing good *ever* comes out of doing drugs. If you don't agree with that statement, then you are probably on drugs.

I knew a businessperson who appeared to be successful. This person had everything you could want—sports cars, million-dollar boats, and summer homes. This individual traveled first class, and most people thought this person was successful. The person I'm talking about even appeared to apply all the principles found in all of the success books. Despite this façade, the individual was not physically healthy. Poor diet and a body polluted with drugs and alcohol led to increased numbers of mistakes. Poor physical health soon resulted in poor mental health, which wound up ruining the individual's personal and professional life. This person, who appeared to be successful to so many, was physically unhealthy, and this caused a deteriorated mental state that eventually destroyed the individual's world.

All too often we hear about professional athletes and celebrities who have it all but succumb to drugs and alcohol and lose everything. Many times "everything" to a celebrity or a professional athlete is an image or reputation. A classic example of a recent celebrity who lost everything is Robert Downey Jr., a highly acclaimed actor. He was nominated for an Academy Award early in his career, but he had an epic and very public collapse due to his voracious addiction to drugs. His addiction is not important; what is important is how the drugs had an obvious impact on his body and mind and almost ruined his career forever. Since he became clean, his career has been resurrected and he is again at the top, with a healthy body and thus a healthy mind.

I have studied many successful people and have been fortunate to have been able to rub elbows with people who have achieved magnificent success. I have never met a truly successful person who pollutes his or her body with drugs or alcohol. I will say that I do have a drink here and there when I'm at a dinner or socializing with some friends, but you won't see me conducting important meetings with a glass of scotch in hand.

FAT PEOPLE DON'T GET HIRED

My editor begged me to remove the above subheading due to a potentially inflammatory response from overweight people. Rather than remove it, I will say it again: *fat people don't get hired.* Employers do not discriminate, but the harsh reality is that *people* do, and science confirms that fat people are not only discriminated against as potential employees, but they are also less likely to climb the corporate ladder within an organization. Despite the fact that nearly 70 percent of the American population is overweight or obese, research confirms that overweight people are less likely to get hired and less likely to get promoted. The research indicates that the perception of fat people is that they are lazy, less competent, indecisive, inactive, disorganized, and not successful. Additional research has shown that employers believe that fat people are more likely to get sick and do not display a good image for the company.

One of the standards by which a person's health is measured is their body mass index (BMI), which is a calculation of height and weight compared to the general population. If a person's BMI is high (generally over twenty-five), research confirms that advancement is negatively impacted.

The fact is that being overweight downright limits your employability; if you are a manual laborer, your prospective employer will wonder if you can keep up or if you will get hurt. If you are in a retail setting, your prospective employer will think twice about the company's corporate image and may not hire an overweight person versus someone who is fit. If an overweight person is lucky enough to get hired, his or her weight and appearance also have a negative impact on placement and promotion.

LOSING WEIGHT AND LOOKING GREAT

A study conducted in 2010 by *Slimming World* found that very overweight workers earn less than their more fit counterparts and were more likely to be passed over for a promotion. A study published in the *Annals of the New York Academy of Sciences* found that "attractiveness" can significantly improve a person's chances of getting hired. The study went on to say that a person's "attractive" appearance creates the impression that the person has greater intelligence and possesses many other social traits that would make him or her a better employee. We discussed appearance earlier, and science confirms it: people who appear to be healthier earn more.

If you are overweight, make the decision today to lose the excess weight. Don't wait until Monday or next week, make the decision *today*. There are many ways to lose weight, and only you can choose what is best for you. I like a couple different books in addition to *Body for Life*; I also recommend *The Health Club Diet* and *Live Disease-Free to 103*. I know both of the latter two authors personally, and we have sold both books together for several years. The customer feedback we get is always positive. You can go to www.diseasefreebook.com and www.healthclubdiet.com to learn more about these two titles.

Regardless of what you do, when you lose weight you feel great, and when you feel great, your attitude becomes great. A healthy self-image goes a long way toward improving your overall life.

ASK FOR MORE FROM YOUR BODY—AND IT MIGHT EVEN GET YOU A BETTER JOB!

When I was in college I interned for a congressman, and we were looking to hire a full-time person to work in our legislative office in Washington, DC. You can imagine how competitive this position was, as people with PhDs, JDs, and MBAs applied for the job. Many had all three! My job was not to judge the résumés, but just to compile them as they came in.

We ultimately hired a young woman who was a member of the bar, and seemed equally as qualified as many of the other résumés that we received. I asked the congressman's chief of staff what set her apart. He said to me that she listed on her résumé that she had completed the New York and Boston Marathons several times. He said that he was an avid runner and that anyone who had the discipline to train for and complete a marathon was obviously someone who was not afraid of hard work, someone who understood how to overcome adversity, and someone who knew how to push through to the finish line. It really hit home with me. We had hundreds of résumés and though most all of them were qualified for the position, this woman got an interview and ultimately the job because of her personal hobbies outside of work.

FROM GINSENG ON RATS TO MILLIONS OF CAPSULES SOLD

When I became involved in the direct response industry almost fifteen years ago, I was just a customer service agent, but my knowledge of health, nutrition, and supplements allowed me to be able to build a rapport with customers and even management. Through hard work I climbed the corporate ladder and became general counsel of a very large direct response company that specialized in selling supplements.

This company had a host of legal challenges that ultimately led to its demise. But my legal education, understanding of sales, and understanding of supplements allowed me to help defend this company and also allowed me to grow as a lawyer and businessperson.

I started Blue Vase in 2009, and we have sold hundreds of millions of capsules of dietary supplements via infomercial. I am the host of most of our infomercials, and my education about dietary supplements combined with my legal background allows me to ask pointed questions that elicit compelling responses. I don't know if I believe in fate or not, but I do think that each event in your life is somehow tied to your future.

My decision to study ginseng with rats is directly related to my success as a lawyer and as a businessperson. My company is the best company in the world that sells supplements via infomercial, and if it weren't for that science fair years ago, maybe I would not be writing this book.

CHAPTER 4
ASK YOURSELF TO INCREASE YOUR VALUE

Unless someone like you cares a whole awful lot / Nothing is going to get better / It's not.

—*Dr. Seuss,* The Lorax

I meant what I said, I said what I meant / An Elephant's faithful, one hundred percent.

—*Horton,* Horton Hatches an Egg

WHY I INCREASED MY VALUE!

When I was a child I was very fortunate to have a loving and caring mother. My mom would read to me almost every night. One story that I remember and that has stuck with me my whole life is *Horton*

Hatches an Egg by Dr. Seuss. This beloved author has touched millions of people, but this story did more than touch me; it changed the way I think. This is not the more common Horton story that most people read, which is *Horton Hears a Who*. Both are great stories. But in *Horton Hatches an Egg*, Horton overcomes adversity, stands up for what he believes in, doesn't care about being a pariah, and most importantly, does what he said he would do.

In the story, Horton the elephant is asked to protect and guard an egg that had a life in it—an awesome responsibility. Horton recognized his responsibility and he followed through with the task that he was given, despite being ridiculed, sitting through rain and sleet, and almost getting killed. He saw it through until the very end. There are so many things to take away from this Horton story, but one of the most important things is that when you are given a task, a job, or a responsibility, you should follow through and do what you say you are going to do. When your task, job, or responsibility seems difficult—even impossible—*ask more* out of yourself. You will be amazed at what you accomplish! And that's the first step you will take to increasing your perceived value to others.

FOOTBALL IN THE RAIN

When I played football as a kid, I noticed a few kids that were just athletically gifted, but I also noticed that those kids always worked harder. Their dads were always at the games and practices, and I would see these kids—yes, kids—jogging the streets, doing sprints after practice, and just working harder. I was a pretty good athlete, but other than being big, I wasn't truly gifted; I always had to work at it. In Pop Warner football we didn't practice every night, and when we didn't I would try to practice on my own. I would try to improve on the skills taught to me the previous week or day. I vividly remember one day putting on my full uniform in a torrential downpour and walking to a field by myself to do wind sprints. I remember feeling a little weird and hoping the other kids didn't see me. But I was building value in me—I was getting faster. Building value in you in whatever you do won't always be easy, but simply doing a little more, trying a little harder, and sometimes going out in the rain will forever build value in *you*.

I GRADUATE FROM COLLEGE . . . NOW WHAT?

After graduating college, my plan of becoming a lawyer was not completely mapped out. I knew that I was tired of being poor, I knew that I had student loans, and I knew that I wanted to begin making money. But with a degree in political science and relatively no work experience, getting a job isn't that easy. After searching for about a month or two I saw a listing in the local paper for a sales job. They had a base salary of $425 a week plus commission. Now this was in 1997, the economy was booming, and people were making a lot of money. The people who were making a lot of money back then were salespeople: they were selling everything from software to stocks, but the big earners were salespeople. There aren't many worse stigmas than that of a car salesman, but I wanted to make money, and even though the economy was booming, I had no experience. So, I responded to the ad in the newspaper and went in for an interview. At that interview I realized that I was being hired not because I had a résumé, but because I had an outgoing personality and seemed likeable. I was excited and nervous at the same time.

My start date wasn't for two weeks, but I went into the dealership a couple days after my interview, grabbed every brochure on every car, and studied them. I remember looking at these brochures and being intimidated and impressed at the same time. Lincoln/Mercury made some great cars. But, to put this into perspective, I couldn't change a tire if you asked me to. In fact, the day I was driving home from college, my Subaru started to overheat, and I had no money and no idea what to do. To my surprise, my little thirteen-year-old brother, who was in the car with me, got under the hood, asked me if I had an eraser—which I did—and he used it to plug something. We put some water in the radiator and we were off. So, the point is that I knew *nothing* about cars.

But if I hadn't responded to that ad, I might not be where I am today. Ford/Lincoln/Mercury trained its employees to not only know how to sell, but also about the products and how to build value in not only the products but in themselves. Many of my friends looked down on the job I had due to the stereotype many people have of car salespeople. But what I was doing was building value in me.

I was a top producer, I made great money, I was learning valuable sales skills, and ultimately I was educating myself about the real world. I met some amazing people selling cars: from professional hockey players to world-renowned architects. I was fascinated with their lifestyles and how they carried themselves. I met people who didn't blink at writing $80,000 checks. I knew that someday I wanted to be where they were.

By this time in my life, I have written much bigger checks. I also made some great friends who are very successful and continue to be. I will discuss rapport building later on in the book, but for now let me just say that most of all, I have built up my brand and my personal value.

STOP GOING TO WORK

One of the things I realized early on in life is that most people don't like to go to work. I could never understand why until recently. When I was a kid I enjoyed work because I got the reward of a paycheck at the end of the week. I enjoyed my paper route, I enjoyed working at Chuck E. Cheese's, I enjoyed working for the Lincoln dealership, I enjoyed working as a recruiter, I enjoyed working as a lawyer, and I love what I do now! Notice, I said, "I love what I do now." I did not say I enjoyed my current "work" or "job."

Larry King made the profound statement, "I haven't worked in fifty-five years!" He continued by saying that when he got up in the morning early in his career, he went to the radio station, he went to CNN, or wherever else. But, according to him, the last time he "worked" was when he delivered packages for UPS at age twenty-one.

Larry King is seventy-seven, and while he no longer has *Larry King Live*, he continues with many other professional endeavors. The key thing to remember is that he considers none of them to be work.

If you are employed, you may not like what you are doing, but one immediate way to increase your *net worth* and your personal productivity is to simply stop going to "work." Though your present situation may not be what you want, until you find something more appealing to you, *stop going to work.*

Wait! Did I just tell you to quit? No, I'm not insane. I am telling you to change your thought process. If you are employed at a factory, then you are going to the [insert the actual name here] factory. If you are employed at a law firm, then you are going to the [insert the actual name here] law firm. If you are employed at a fast-food restaurant, then you are going to the [insert the actual name here] fast-food restaurant. Change your place of employment from something you refer to as "work" into an actual place you go to learn skills and improve the quality of your product. Change your "job" into a place you go that puts food in your family's mouths and allows you to afford the things you like. If you do that, you will no longer be thinking of yourself as "working." Instead, you will be contributing to the company and increasing your personal *net worth*.

If you are not employed and are looking to land a job, then stop looking for "work." Start looking for a way to improve your life. Look for an actual place of employment that will get you off unemployment benefits and provide you and your family with stability. Too many people look for the ideal "job" or hold out for something better.

Though I believe it is a good idea to try to find something you are passionate about, I would urge you to stop looking for "work." Once you start to look for a place where you can improve your quality of life, then many more doors will begin to open, and you will find employment faster than you imagined.

Once you quit going to "work," you will find that whatever you do becomes fulfilling and meaningful. It may not be your first choice of employment, but that is okay. So stop working, and start looking for a place that will get you to where you want to go. Only you can make the decision—today—that you no longer *work* anywhere.

My company has close to 150 employees, and although I do not know everyone, I can say with confidence that my executives don't come to "work." They come to a place where they contribute, grow, and improve not only their *net worth* but also the company's productivity. How do I know this? Well, my executive team is on the job 24/7, and most of them tell me that they love coming in to the office. Every day we are faced with adversity and challenges, and we work through them, but we are never "working"; we are all a part of something special. You too can be a part of something special; you just need to change the way you think about your employment.

Finally, be proud of what you do. I don't care if you clean septic tanks or run a Fortune 500 company; every career is honorable, and you need to be proud of it. Take pride in what you do at your place of employment. At my company I have a fairly large call center, with people taking incoming calls for sales and customer service. My salespeople at Blue Vase Marketing are titled sales professionals.

They are not call center reps, and they take pride in what they do. My customer service agents are customer satisfaction professionals who don't just serve customers—they provide customer satisfaction. All of my employees take pride in what they do. If they don't, or they can't internalize the principles that are in not only this book but also instilled in our staff, then they will not be employed at Blue Vase Marketing very long.

WHY TO INCREASE YOUR VALUE!

When I was selling cars there were a couple of lot boys or lot guys. One was a kid named Max. Max was about nineteen, had just dropped out of college, and was just floating through life. Max was very smart, and he knew everything about these cars. He could tell you everything from how much they weighed to their gas mileage. He also knew about every other car on the planet. Max was making $9 an hour, while some salespeople were making six figures. One day one of the senior sales guys told him he should sell cars. Max was reluctant and a bit nervous. He wasn't a "salesman."

Well, Max decided to give it a shot. He went through the two-week training period, and on his *first* day on the sales floor he sold *five* cars. He made in a day what he normally made in two weeks, parking cars. It wasn't beginner's luck either; Max went on to sell *lots* of cars and made a bunch of money. After selling cars for a while and really learning how to sell, Max *asked*, what more could he sell? Well, Max went on to the mortgage business and was making *high* six figures—only a few years after he was earning $9 an hour! Today, Max is a very close friend of mine and is a top executive at Monster.com, where he has a team working under him and where he makes more money than 99 percent of the American public. Most important, he has a beautiful family, a nice house, and is very happy. And it's all because Max built value in himself.

There was another lot boy who worked with Max, and he was a great guy. But, that is all he saw for his future. He thought he would always be a lot boy, and last I heard, he still is. Actually, this guy is not a "boy"; he is a grown man with a family and was barely making it. He just never decided to increase his personal value. He was afraid of failing. Sometimes you have to be defeated to build value in you. *Ask* yourself: Would you rather park the cars, or sell them?

HOW TO BUILD VALUE IN *YOU*

Too many of us are concerned with our dollars-and-cents compensation. After all, the economy is a mess, and we are having trouble making ends meet. However, if you understand my techniques, your "compensation" will increase in ways you would have never imagined. Just recently, I hired Nate as an unpaid intern for my information technology department. Nate came to us on his own initiative while he was working on a certificate program that does not offer school credits. He was not attending a college, and he was not asking to get paid. He simply took it upon himself to take a course that would teach him a new skill. I knew Nate had drive and was focused.

Nate joined our IT team, and there was no task he would not do. He took it upon himself to learn about all of our systems and procedures. During this *unpaid* internship, Nate was increasing his net worth. The more he learned how to do things at my company, the more valuable he became. There was an instance when we needed *everyone* to jump on the phones at my call center and make sales, and Nate had never "sold" anything in his life. But not only did Nate do this task, he did it with noticeable enthusiasm and outsold some of my sales professionals.

As you can imagine, we hired Nate, and as an hourly employee he continued to increase his net worth. He learned how to take customer service calls. He learned how to install video systems. Nate would do anything we asked of him. He doesn't think anything is beneath him (or above him, for that matter). One time, Nate installed cameras in our warehouse until 3:00 a.m. because he knew we needed them. Nate was given a private office and is making a salary people would kill for. He continued to increase his wealth, and over time the actual dollars will start to grow in his bank account.

You see, Nate thought a little differently. He understands that we as his employer aren't just offering him a job; we have given him an opportunity to grow and learn and at the same time have a steady income. Nate actually left Blue Vase to start his own IT firm. I must say I was sad to see him go, but proud at the same time. Nate built value in himself by taking the course he did, getting the internship with us, and constantly improving. Nate would not be where he is today if not for the way he thought and his continual self-improvement. Building value in *you* today will increase your *net worth* tomorrow.

Nate is just one example, and I could fill this entire book with more examples of how fortunate I am to have great employees. They increased their value by increasing *my* value and the value of the company. The night I started my company, my chief information officer, Chris, and I were up all night programming phones, because without phones we could not cover the calls. Our now-office manager and my amazing assistant Shauna (really our chief operating officer) came to the office at midnight with an air mattress and pillows. On another occasion, one Friday night at 8:00 p.m., Shauna took it upon herself to spot-test some of our systems and found they weren't working. If she had not checked the system (a process that someone else usually does), we would have lost, conservatively, $70,000. Shauna literally knows every aspect of the business and if asked to do something, she can help out with any area of the company. Every one of my employees, when hired, is required to spend some time in every department. We do this to help them learn and understand how each division works and how together they must become a team. This also improves their value to the company. We also require each new hire to read *The Go-Getter* by Peter Kyne and *The Fred Factor* by Mark Sanborn. Both of these books have been instrumental in my success and the success of my companies. I recommend that you read them.

A DEPOSIT IN THE EMOTIONAL BANK ACCOUNT

Several years ago, when I was a full-time lawyer and general counsel of another company, I was looking to hire an intern in my legal department. I went to the human resources department and asked them to help me find one. I received a couple of résumés that were okay, but nothing excited me or seemed like a fit. A few weeks into my search, I was told that there was a candidate in the foyer waiting to speak with me. I was a little shocked, since I did not have an interview set up. I asked my assistant to greet this individual and investigate. Well, apparently this young man saw our ad, took it upon himself to fill out an application, and was interested in meeting with me.

I looked at his résumé and was impressed. He was a licensed attorney, he had some decent experience, and he went to a decent law school. So, for my own amusement and curiosity, I granted him an interview. To my surprise, he was well dressed, polite, articulate, and *perfect*. I even had a colleague interview this young man to make sure that my instincts were correct. However, I wasn't hiring an attorney. I told him I was looking for an intern and couldn't possibly pay him an adequate salary. Well, guess what? I hired him on the spot. He went on to work for me for several years and made six figures at the end of his tenure with the firm. I was so impressed by his performance that I then hired him at Blue Vase Marketing. He was always on time, stayed late, and had his work complete. In addition, he also took it upon himself to improve the department. I later found out that he originally sent me a personal letter, but human resources had intercepted it.

Right from the very beginning, this young man made a huge deposit into my emotional bank account. I knew that he was not afraid to take risks, that he was a go-getter, and that he was a hard worker, just by the way he showed up in a suit to fill out an application and asking to speak with me. Can you imagine? Some people may have been offended, but not me. He started out with a full bank account with me, and I was willing to invest in him. Today he is an integral part of my business and I trust him with making business decisions on my behalf. He came quite a long way from being basically an intern to helping with major business decisions.

RISE TO A CHALLENGE

My old boss had a side project that he needed some help with. His family owned some property on a very private and wealthy island in New England. His neighbor had filed for a variance that, if granted, would have obstructed my boss's beachfront property and diminished the value of the land. I knew nothing about real estate, property, or maritime law, but I spent countless hours researching the law and ways to prevent his neighbor from encroaching on his family's property. The challenge was that his neighbor was and is a very powerful real estate lawyer! Of course, I am always up for a good challenge.

ACTION: the act by which we incorporate our goals, dreams, ideas, and imagination, turning them into a reality through persistent effort.

One thing that I discovered when I was researching the area was that the shoreline was very unique; it is the only place in the world with a particular type of rock. I found a document from the 1800s in a library in Texas that substantiated the rarity of this type of rock. In addition to several other arguments, I was able to prevent the neighbor from building and ruining my boss's family's property due to the rarity of this rock and the potential destruction of the ecology. I did this for no monetary gain, but you can bet that this *action* was a huge deposit in his emotional bank account.

DON'T ADD DEBT TO THE EMOTIONAL BANK ACCOUNT

Withdrawals from the emotional bank account can cause emotional overdrafts, which incur fines and fees. How can this happen? If you are late, if you take advantage of your boss's kindness, if you don't do more than what is asked of you, or if you don't finish a job you are asked to do—you're running in the red. Just watch that emotional bank account deplete. It can empty faster than deposits are made.

Deposits that improve your balance in your boss's bank account:

> Be early.
> Stay late.
> Work on your days off (if necessary).
> Support your boss's objectives with sound advice.
> Complete tasks early and make sure they are correct.
> Never speak badly about anyone in the office or your place of employment.
> Be a team player.
> Don't point out your accomplishments (with some exceptions: see the following); they will be noticed.
> Don't expect something in return for doing more than what is asked of you.
> Be likeable and improve your social skills. Eighty-five percent of all people are hired because they are liked.
> Show your bosses respect at all times and *never* speak badly of them.

Just these few things will get you further in your place of employment and make you more valuable to your company. But not doing them—or running up overdrafts—will have the opposite result.

I had an employee who started with me the day I opened my doors. She was capable and willing to do anything. She was educated, likeable, and hardworking. However, she had a tendency to always be absent after a big athletic event. It didn't matter if it was the Ryder Cup or the Final Four; she was sick the next day. It became comical; if the Red Sox were playing the Yankees on a Tuesday night, she was sick on Wednesday.

I think she realized that I began to take notice, so she said things like, "I will make up the hours on Saturday." Of course, she never did. That is like hitting your debit card for the purchase of a car when your balance is zero! I spoke to her. She said she would not let it happen in the future, but it continued, and though I didn't fire her immediately, the emotional bank account was drained and she had no credit lines to tap into at the end.

Finally, she was out for *ten* days without an email, a phone call, a text, a letter, *nothing*. We called her home and her husband said she was really ill, but why didn't he think to call us? This woman held the title of vice president at my company, yet she couldn't call someone or have her husband call to say she was on her deathbed? Every time I called, her phone was dead!

We aren't in high school, and "the dog ate my homework" excuse doesn't work in the real world. It was brought to my attention by the young lawyer just referenced that a local lodge (in which she was very active) just happened to be on a cruise in the Bahamas during the exact same time she was out! Now, I never confirmed that she was on that ship, but the circumstantial evidence surely pointed in that direction. Sick for ten days at the same time as a cruise, with a dead cell phone and *no* communication? Either way, I fired her for job abandonment. This is an extreme example of depleting the emotional bank account. Her constant debits of absenteeism after sporting events and failing to make up her missed hours overdrafted the emotional bank account and ultimately maxed out all the lines of credit she had.

DON'T CONFUSE ACTIVITY WITH ACCOMPLISHMENT

Blue Vase Marketing is a decent-size company. Our employee base changes, but it's always over one hundred employees. We have offices in Boston and Chicago, and we are expanding to London. Some analysts would call us a small business, but I would beg to differ.

Several years ago I implemented a daily and weekly update program in which my key executives and some supporting staff send me daily reports on what they did the day before, weekly reports on the prior week, *and* what they plan on accomplishing the next day and the following week. Some of my executives were not excited about this, and I even had a few ask for my rationale. Well, the good news for me is that I am in the corner office for a reason, and as my mother used to say to me when I asked her why I couldn't do something, my response was, "Because I said so"—kind of.

But the real reason for this reporting system is that I learned in my business career that too many people confuse activity with accomplishment. Employees can get caught up doing tasks with zero benefit for the company. My daily reports allow me to monitor their activity *and* accomplishments. Activity is the busy work that people do in order to accomplish a goal. Accomplishment is the finalization and completion of the goal. One thing that I discussed with my executives about the reports is that they allow me to see what has been accomplished. But, it also allows *them* to see what they accomplished. When you write things down and reflect on the previous day, if you realize you did not accomplish something, then you know that your day was essentially wasted and you should be able to see it. I help them recognize this and also point them in the right direction.

So, whether you are working on your business or personal life, *ask* yourself, what did you accomplish today, and last week. Then what do you plan on accomplishing tomorrow and next week. Let me also say that in your personal life your accomplishments can be really small and you don't have to change the world every day, sometimes just relaxing is an accomplishment. If your goal for the next day is to just relax, then accomplish that task, and if you didn't then figure out why and *ask* how you can accomplish that goal the next day. When you recognize that you did or didn't accomplish your daily goal, you will become so much more efficient and you will find that you will have a lot more time to accomplish even more things.

Recently I hired someone for my executive team who is very organized and is what most people would consider a type-A personality. But this person is a bit over the top and takes on too much "work." I have had to have a few conversations with this individual, reminding him that taking on too much *activity* will not lead to *accomplishment* of the main objective. He is very smart, a hard worker, and cares about what he does. But, at the end of the day, none of that matters. If you have a position at a company and you have a goal or an objective, even if it is not well defined, you must find a way to ensure that you have accomplished something of value. The same goes for your personal life. Going to the gym and sitting in the sauna will not lead to weight loss. The *activity* of going to the gym is not what *accomplishes* the goal of weight loss and good health. The *activity* of actually exercising is what will *accomplish* your goal.

YOU NEED TO BRING ATTENTION TO YOURSELF— IT'S OKAY

After another discussion with the aforementioned executive and a little more direction from me, his accomplishments have exceeded my expectations. But that only happened because he made me aware that his activity actually *was* an accomplishment. I needed to understand what he was actually doing as his job is very technical. The moral of this part of the story is that you should *ask* yourself, "Do my superiors actually know what I'm accomplishing?" If not, you need to find a way to make sure they know what you are doing and what you have done. Even though I see daily and weekly reports, I was still confused as to what he was doing, but after having our last talk and educating myself, I realized that his work was top-notch!

I DESERVE TO BE SUCCESSFUL—THE PROOF IS IN THE PERSONAL PROFILE

I will never forget the day I bought my first real suit at Men's Wearhouse. It was 1997, and it was very exciting. I was fresh out of college and selling Lincoln/Mercury cars, and I cashed my first commission check of $1,507. For a young man who had come from the other side of the tracks with nothing, this felt like a million dollars. The most my mother had made for a whole year was $18,000.

So, I walked in with a goal of buying a really nice suit for no more than $500. Mind you, I had never purchased a suit before, or anything else—other than my first car—for more than $500. The salesperson greeted me: "Hello, sir. Welcome to Men's Wearhouse." He must have seen me coming from a hundred miles away with cash in my pocket. It was as if he had X-ray vision and was counting my greenbacks. He fitted me with a beautiful navy blue suit, a 46-athletic. Man, it looked good! I thought I was done there. But I wasn't even close.

"Before you meet with the tailor," the salesman stated, "try on this pair of shoes."

"I don't need shoes," I responded. To which he replied, "Well try them on, so when we meet with the tailor we can get a better fit."

I was wearing sneakers. So I reluctantly tried on a shiny pair of burgundy shoes that perfectly matched my suit. "I'm not buying a $75 pair of shoes," I assured him. "I already hit my cap of $500."

He looked at me and said, "Mike, you wouldn't drive a new car with old tires would you?" Well, you already know my answer: I walked out of that store with a suit, shoes, and a couple of nice ties—just over $700 in clothes. I felt great and couldn't wait to wear my new suit and those shiny shoes. Funny thing—I still have those shoes, and guess what? Those shoes have made me millions of dollars.

The lesson: Pay attention to your attire. Your clothes and shoes and the quality of the shoes project to others that you care, that you are on your game and ready for the task at hand. Any self-improvement book or publication worth reading will tell you to invest in your attire. When you dress for success, you will be successful. When you are at your current job and you wear a suit or a nice blouse and skirt, people notice.

In *The Magic of Thinking Big*, David Schwartz spends a lot of time on this subject, and in *The Strangest Secret* (check this out before you read *The Secret* by Rhonda Byne), Earl Nightengale says, "You become what you think about." Well, when you are dressed for success, you become who you think you are. When you dress like someone important, you will begin to act important. When you act important, people begin to treat you like the VIP you know you are. When you are a VIP you will rise to the top.

Recently, I was visiting a local coffee shop/country store and overheard a woman named Betty tell a story proving this simple strategy. Betty told her friends about a colleague named Sue who had jury duty. Sue decided it was appropriate to dress up in her "business attire" for jury duty. Well, Sue went to jury duty and was dismissed early. Sue then decided to remain dressed in her "business attire" at her place of employment. That day, Betty noticed Sue was more productive; her work quality improved and she seemed happier. Others in the business treated Sue as though she were upper management. Unfortunately, Sue didn't fully grasp what happened and returned the next day in her old clothes, going back to being unhappy and doing just enough to get by.

Your attire will not only change your attitude and your productivity but will also increase your *net worth*—guaranteed.

And the opposite is most definitely true. One day I walked into my office and was greeted by our wonderful receptionist when I noticed a disheveled young man sitting in our waiting area. He looked as if he had taken his clothes from the bottom of his laundry basket, rolled out of bed, put on his sneakers, and arrived at my office. I inquired of my assistant who he was, as it appeared he was in need of help.

She told me he was at my company for an interview for one of our internship programs with the information technology department. Thoughts flashed through my mind: "No person who dresses like that for an interview will be allowed to touch a doorknob at this company, let alone a computer." I went to my chief information officer and told him to sit this young man down in our beautiful conference room and explain to him immediately why we were not even going to consider his application, and then to hand him a copy of *The Go-Getter* and *The Fred Factor*.

I thought it was a generous offer. Remarkably, he stormed out of the conference room, ran outside of our office, and threw the books at our doors while voicing a loud series of expletives. He may be the next Bill Gates or Steve Jobs, but I never would know that by the way he appeared or acted. Because of his poor personal profile, he was never even given the chance to reach his potential at Blue Vase Marketing. I hope someday he grows from that experience and it will be fruitful when he interviews for his next position.

When I played college football at Springfield College, I never understood why we dressed up to go to the locker room on game day. After all, we were just going to change into a uniform that was going to get very filthy. It didn't make sense, but I did it because I had to. Then one day it clicked.

We had a home game and for home games, depending on how far the opposing team had to travel, they arrived either the day of the game or the day before. I can't remember the team, but I remember watching them exit the bus. Every player had a tie on, some had a suit, others had a blazer, but they all looked like they were ready for business. I remember looking into the eyes of a few players and they all looked back at me with the confidence of being ready for the task. And at that moment I respected them as persons and as a team—not an opponent.

When we traveled to opposing teams we had uniforms we wore constantly. By the way, this habit translates well into professions that have a uniform. Our uniforms—wind pants and a jacket—were burgundy with white lettering. You could not get on the bus if you did not have your proper attire, and some athletes stayed back because they were not dressed properly. Our uniforms showed solidarity—we were a team *and* we cared how we looked. It is intimidating to the opposing side when the entire bus of football players steps out looking sharp and all wearing the same thing. I may have only played for division two and division three, but it didn't matter—we had a dress code, detailed down to our cleats. If anyone was out of dress code, they couldn't even stand on the sidelines. Plus, our football uniforms had to look nice while playing! Seems crazy, but this proven concept of looking good when you are playing a sport has a direct impact on the quality of play. Try it—it will also improve the quality of your work.

Have you ever observed a military platoon that looked all disheveled? No, not unless they were on the battlefield. Their uniforms have a standard: their shoes are so shiny you can see the soldiers' reflections. If they have medals, they shine so brightly that if the sun reflects off just right you could be blinded. In addition, their uniforms have more starch than a plate of potatoes. Our military and virtually every military around the world understands the importance of looking good. If you don't care what you look like, then you won't care about the task at hand.

Whether you are a home team walking to your locker room on game day or you are dressing for success at work, it shows others you mean business and it tells your subconscious you are about to do something very important. When you are dressed nicely, people respect you and view you differently.

Tomorrow, whether you have a job or are unemployed, I want you to put on your nicest attire and wear it proudly. Make sure your shirt is ironed, your pants or skirt are wrinkle-free, and your shoes are the best pair you have. If you're wearing a suit, make sure it is lint-free and that your tie is perfectly tied and centered. Some people may snicker—hand them a copy of my book. Observe how others treat you. If your job doesn't permit you to do this at work, then I want you to get dressed up in your nicest attire and go to the mall. Just walk into stores, sit down at the food court, and observe how others look at you. Observe how you feel. At first this may seem uncomfortable. Don't worry; most people in the mall don't know you. I guarantee you will have a great day and want to dress the same way each day moving forward.

I hope I made this point clear. Dress like someone important. You will act important and you will be treated like you are important. This goes for any situation in any place of employment. If you work in a factory and have a uniform, make sure it is clean and pressed; if you work at a fast-food chain, make sure your uniform looks brand new. When I was a kid I was fortunate to get a job at Chuck E. Cheese's. This beginning job taught me many things about business and how to act in a business environment. My experience was over twenty years ago, and Chuck E. Cheese's is still thriving. I worked in the kitchen, and our uniform was a red shirt, a hat, khaki pants, and white shoes. I made sure my pants were always clean, my shirt was ironed, and my shoes were clean. This can be difficult when you are working in a kitchen. But, at fifteen, I was well respected by management, became a kitchen team leader, and regularly received raises without asking. Your appearance speaks not only to the people who are looking at you; it also speaks to your conscious and subconscious mind, letting both of them know that you *are*.

TIP: Don't know how to tie a tie? Go to YouTube.com; there are dozens of great videos. I even watched YouTube to learn how to tie a Windsor knot!

TIP: Spend more and buy less. You will find that buying a quality suit and quality shoes will go much further than buying multiple suits and shoes for the same price.

COMPLIMENT YOUR PEERS WITH SINCERITY

A sincere compliment to your peers goes a long way in the work-a-day world. When a woman changes a hairstyle and you genuinely like it, or when a colleague has a sharp suit on, there is nothing wrong with saying things like, "Linda, I like what you have done with your hair. It looks great," "Sarah, that is a terrific suit. You look great in red," "Jason, that blazer looks sharp," "John, nice tie. I like the color," "Skip, those are some really nice shoes," or, "Shauna, that is a nice suit."

People appreciate being noticed, and they will reciprocate. Ultimately, they will like being around you, and if you are their boss, they will work harder for you. Now unfortunately, in today's age people are *very* concerned with sexual harassment and political correctness. Sometimes, even basic compliments can be misinterpreted. So I advise you to use this technique with caution.

BE SOCIAL—NOT JUST WITH MEDIA

It seems that just as technology begins to make our lives easier it also makes us more introverted. Next time you are in a mall, notice that more than half of the people have their head down—looking at their smartphones. Go into a bar and you will spot dozens of people oblivious to their surroundings, texting or playing games on their phones. When you are in an elevator, take notice of how many people are looking down at their phones.

One of the best ways to gain an opportunity for employment is through your social circles. The good jobs are never in the help wanted section of newspapers or listed on the job boards. One lawyer who worked for me for a while also happens to be a very good friend from high school, and although I'm not a fan of nepotism, I hired him. I had not seen him for a while, but I met another friend out for dinner and a couple of drinks, and, lo and behold, my old high school buddy—who is extremely smart—was looking for something more than what he was doing. I told him that I had an opening. After going through an interview—more like just catching up and discussing what the position required—I hired him, and he is doing an amazing job. He hit the ground running and has made positive changes for my company.

I'm not suggesting that you go to your local pub looking for a job, but I am suggesting that you get out of the house, put away your phone, tablet, PC, or whatever device you now use to communicate, and start talking to people. Last time I checked, people still have to talk to each other at some point in order to get things done.

BECOME A MEMBER OF YOUR LOCAL BNI GROUP

Business Network International (BNI) is an organization that gets people together in their respective communities in a professional setting. The costs are minimal, and many times you can tag along with a friend. Their mission statement explains it all: "The mission of BNI is to help members increase their business through a structured, positive, and professional 'word-of-mouth' program that enables them to develop long-term, meaningful relationships with quality business professionals." There you will meet people in your community who are successful, and many times these people are employers looking for quality people. You can go to www.bni.com to learn more about the organization, and I highly recommend doing so. No matter what your profession or trade, from carpentry to dentistry, joining a local BNI group will certainly provide you with more opportunities. There are several other organizations, like Toastmasters, which also increase your social circle. Toastmasters is also inexpensive and a great organization where you can meet successful people in your area and improve your communication skills. Their website is www.toastmasters.org. Other organizations to increase your prospective employment opportunities are the Shriners, Lions Club, and the Masonic Lodge. Not only do these organizations do wonderful things for the community, but many of their members are also professionals in your area.

EXPLOIT OPPORTUNITY

Any time you are given an opportunity at your employment, whatever it is, take it on with enthusiasm and give that opportunity your absolute best. When working in the kitchen at Chuck E. Cheese's when I was a kid, I noticed there were different tasks that were more important. Only management made the dough, the key ingredient and foundation of the pizza. At the time I was allowed to make the pizzas, prep them, and prepare other food selections. I was also allowed to help in many other areas of the kitchen as the pizza chef as well. But then one morning I was given the opportunity—in the following I discuss the difference between an opportunity and responsibility—to work with my manager at making and kneading the dough. The process is more complex than simply mixing water and flour, and I was given an opportunity to learn. Over time, I learned the process and very soon, I was given the responsibility of making the dough—again increasing my *net worth*. By the time I left Chuck E. Cheese's at seventeen, I was running the kitchen. This may seem trivial, but I realized that when given an opportunity to learn more about a current employer, you should do it; you become more valuable to the organization.

I often hear, "I wasn't hired for that," or "I went to college and shouldn't be doing that" from the Y generation, and it scares me to think about what that generation will be like in the future and how they will run this country.

OPPORTUNITY: a situation created by you that allows you to achieve *your goals*.

About a year ago, I made it mandatory that every person in my office learn how to make a sale on the phone. Everyone from Nate and Chris in information technology to the people in my accounting department had to learn how to make a sale. Why did I do this? Sure, I wanted to increase our productivity, but I was also giving everyone an *opportunity*, in addition to testing my employees' drive and willingness to be a part of the team.

Unbeknownst to me, my accountant—whose office was across the hall from mine—packed up everything in his office and left for the night. He came back the next day and worked, but I didn't go in his office until a few nights later, when I discovered that his office was stripped of all personal belongings. I called him in a panic, and he told me that he did that because he felt it was beneath him to "take sales calls," and that this was not why he went to college. I explained to him that by taking sales calls it would give him a better idea of our operations, possibly improve our profitability, and ultimately increase his net worth. Then I fired him.

Ask yourself this question: "If I were the boss, what would I do?" You see, if you think you are too good for something, or if when called upon to help you do so begrudgingly, you hurt yourself and the company. There is a school of thought in the business world that executives shouldn't get their hands dirty. That is a risky business philosophy and increases the gap between subordinates and executives; in essence, the guys at the top lose touch with reality. I do everything—I take customer service calls, I take out the trash, I make coffee or copies when necessary. It keeps me in touch with my company.

When you think like the boss, you may someday become the boss. When given an opportunity, embrace it, exploit it, and learn from it to increase your *net worth*! No task is too big or too small.

TAKE ON ADDITIONAL RESPONSIBILITY

If you merely want to get by, I am sorry for that. But if you are reading this book, I believe it's because you desire more from life. If you are given additional responsibilities, embrace them. Additional responsibility and opportunities may overlap. But additional responsibility is generally a task that is an extension or a part of your current career. For example, when I hired a lawyer who works in my legal department (the buddy I ran into at the local pub), his responsibility was contracts and compliance. He did not have a lot of legal experience, but in just under a year, he handled every aspect of my business that has any legal implication—which, by the way, is *everything*!

I gave him the opportunity to learn the different facets of my business and entrusted him with this responsibility. I gave him the opportunity to make a few sales calls to understand the sales process, so that he could better serve the company and increase his knowledge and *net worth*. Each day that went by he increased his *value* to the company and his personal *net worth*. You see, his additional responsibility is also a bigger opportunity to learn different aspects of the law while being employed, *and* it makes him more valuable to the company.

I mentioned the story of my dad and the technique he used to increase his net worth during tough economic times in a television advertisement for my book. My dad is a machinist and almost sixty-two. He has been with the same company for almost ten years but has always just been a machinist. I used to discuss with him that I thought he should try to climb the ladder and become a foreman or a shift supervisor, but he was nervous about "rocking the boat." You see, his environment seemed pretty oppressive, or at least this is what I perceived it to be like.

Recently, his company, like many others, experienced significant layoffs. He watched his peers get fired or laid off, and to make matters worse, my dad came down with Bell's palsy, which required him to take a temporary leave of absence. When I was discussing my book with my dad, he asked me what he should do. I told him to do two things. Number one, take on more responsibility, and number two, exploit any opportunity given to him. I told him that most people, when surrounded with doom and gloom, wait around like cattle standing to be slaughtered. I told my dad that if he applied these two very basic and simple techniques, he would increase his personal *net worth* and eventually even increase his pay, despite others being let go.

My dad decided to take an active role in a safety committee at work. This was an opportunity he had been given a while ago, but this time he exploited the opportunity. He told me about a meeting he was in, and how the new chief operating officer took notice and began to seek my dad's advice.

Just being on the safety committee was an opportunity. After I explained more of the *Ask More, Get More* techniques, he has become the lead man in the safety committee and additional upper management has taken notice. During this downtime my father made the decision to work *even harder* and longer than he has in the past. Sometimes, he is working when he is not even on the clock.

He also decided to take on more responsibility without being asked. He took it upon himself to help others around him and to take on more tasks for himself. I am happy to say that my dad now feels more secure than ever. He is not worried about losing his job and, God forbid, even if he were to lose it, he is now more valuable to other prospective employers. He can even use these experiences as part of his interview process. These are very simple, easy, and effective ways to increase your *net worth* in any job, and this works in any industry.

INTERVIEWING

There are entire books and courses dedicated to the employment interview process. The interview is your first step to getting hired and should be taken very seriously. But I just want to say a few things about it here, since in an interview you also have a chance to increase your value, and there are specific ways to do it.

Earlier I mentioned my confident—some would say cocky—attitude while interviewing. It is important to be careful not to cross the line from confidence to cockiness. If you appear to be cocky or act like a know-it-all, then you will not get hired. However, someone who is confident has a better shot.

One very important thing you need to do *prior* to your interview is to set up a few mock interviews with your friends or family members and treat this mock interview as if it were the real thing. Create a realistic setting; if possible, use a conference room or a desk. Dress as if you were at the interview, and have your résumé ready and with you. If you have a camera, record the interview and see if you have a nervous twitch, repeat yourself, or say "umm" constantly. Practice the interview before the real thing, so that you are prepared to answer the tough questions. Most important, you will be more comfortable with the interview process, as interviews can be intimidating.

Tips:

› Always wear a suit to an interview.

› Always be positive, even when discussing your previous employment.

› Be confident but not cocky.

› Be prepared.

› Know the company you are interviewing with.

A TIME TO JUST BE

When I was a young lawyer a family member said to me one day that I was a lawyer now and I should start acting like one. What does a lawyer act like? There are plenty of jokes that answer that question, but just because I was now a lawyer I was not going to *be* someone else.

I went to law school nights at Suffolk University in Boston. My first night in class the professor asked us to introduce ourselves. There were about 150 students in the class, and most of them were working professionals in Boston. Most were at major law firms, many had degrees from Harvard, Cornell, MIT, or Boston University, and seemed very serious. When it came to me, I said, "My name is Mike, I sell cars at North Shore Lincoln Mercury in Peabody, and if anyone needs a car, come see me." The whole room broke out in laughter, and I must admit I was a little embarrassed. But, I was just being *me*. After that introduction I had several students approach me and tell me how much they enjoyed my candor and thought what I said was humorous. But one guy who approached me ended up becoming one of my closest friends. He later told me that he knew from what I said that I was a good guy and wasn't fake. Which is true; I was just being *me*! I made a lifelong friend who is very successful in his own world, and it may have never happened if I wasn't just *me*. And by the way . . . I ended up selling two cars to two of my classmates.

A few months ago in one of my Bikram yoga classes, at the end, when we were essentially meditating, the instructor said that sometimes we have to just be. Most people would define my personality as a type-A: one who is always going and doing things and just pushing forward. But sometimes you have to just *be*. I had a real hard time conceptualizing what that really means. After actually discussing this with many people, I came to understand that just *being* is just being you, taking notice of who you are, and just focusing on the small things in life. It is also understanding who you are as a person. As we age, we grow individually, and knowing yourself and who you are evolves. But, sometimes stepping back and just *being* is crucial to understanding where you want to go and what you want to do. I am very fortunate that I can just *be* essentially when I want. *Ask More, Get More* is not only about financial freedom and success, but it is also about *you* being able to be *you*.

When you are having a tough day, step back and just *be*. It may actually be one of the greatest ways to increase your perceived value.

PART II

ASK MORE FROM OTHERS

CHAPTER 5

BE PREPARED TO ASK FOR MORE

"KNOW" BEFORE THEY SAY "NO"—HOW TO GET READY FOR THE BATTLE FOR MORE!

Why are we afraid of being sold goods and services? Why are salespeople considered bad people? We live in a society and world that buys and sells things. People in other countries and cultures hard-sell things to each other every day. If you have ever been to a tropical island or a major city in other countries, street vendors constantly try to sell you their goods. It is just a way of life.

In upcoming chapters, I discuss negotiation and how we, as human beings, also resist the activity of negotiation. But, when we *buy* something, *pay* for something, *purchase* something, or *sell* something, most of us are uneasy or get nervous about these activities. The fact is, since the beginning of time we have *bought, sold, paid for,* and *purchased* things one way or another. Buying and selling things has made the world go round since the beginning of time.

Before currency, we bartered: "I will give you three sheep for your cow." The bartering system inherently had negotiation built into it. There wasn't really a set value for a pig or a cow. For example, does a barren cow have more or less value than one that could give birth to a calf? It all depends on what you want the cow to do. So, if you had a barren cow and you wanted to sell it, you would have to negotiate with the other party and convince them as to why that barren cow was good for the buyer, and conversely, the other person involved would have to convince you why they want to pay less for your cow, and that their commodity was worth more to you than you were asking.

Though the concept of bartering has been lost in modern economies like the United States, all over the world there are companies where you can *get* things for only the cost of your skills. For instance, if you are a lawyer and you need to have your cabinets refinished, you can go to places like SwapRight.com, where you essentially trade your services. There are many different types of companies similar to the above example. It is *free* to join and you can get things done without actually exchanging money.

3 P'S + 1 P

So if buying and selling has been around forever, then why are people still so afraid of it? The real answer is that we do not trust salespeople and we also lack confidence in ourselves. One very important technique that will alleviate the fear of being taken advantage of by what you may perceive as an unscrupulous salesperson is my "3 P's + 1 P" technique: *Prepare, prepare, prepare + prepare* one more time. Prepare for the purchase by researching everything possible about the item you intend to purchase. Once you have exhausted this tactic, prepare for it again as if you didn't do it before. Repeat that one more time, and then finally, *prepare again.* Seems unnecessary, right? Well, it isn't. Successful people, wealthy people, and happy people are prepared for whatever comes their way. 3 P's + 1 P will improve your success rate in anything you do.

The book *Outliers* by Malcolm Gladwell edified my method by attempting to find the common denominators in successful people. One thing that seemed to be clear was that in order to be successful in anything, you need to put in 10,000 hours worth of work. Gladwell goes on to discuss professional athletes, businessmen like Bill Gates, and musicians like the Beatles. They all prepared for their success. The Beatles played almost every day all over Europe for two years before anyone knew who they were. Bill Gates was programming computers in middle school. Being prepared eliminates the fear of being "sold." It also eliminates the fear of buying things and feeling bad about it. You will no longer think, "did I pay too much," "is this the best brand," or, "do I need this item?" Many of us get what we call "buyer's remorse," which ruins the positive experience of buying things. If you apply the 3 P's + 1 P technique in any situation, whether buying, selling, taking an exam, or preparing for a meeting, you will ultimately be more successful and fulfilled. And if you are the type of person who just wings it and you still get by, then by using my system of 3 P's + 1 P, you will achieve more success than you ever imagined.

I am a licensed attorney in the Commonwealth of Massachusetts, but in order to become licensed you need to pass the bar exam, a test that many say is the most difficult standardized test among professionals. It is certainly not an exam where you can just wing it (unless you are Leonardo DiCaprio in the film *Catch Me If You Can*). I had the unpleasant experience of not passing the bar exam by the margin of a single question. When it's that close, the entire exam goes before committees to review again to make sure the results are correct. And supposedly you usually get "bumped up" and they pass you. Well, that did not happen to me; I did not pass the bar exam.

Two weeks before the exam, I was talking with a friend of mine around 11:00 in the evening in the local library. My friend told me how he could literally recall his notes that he had taken over the past *eleven weeks*. I said to myself, "Eleven weeks!" I had only been studying for about three weeks, and that was during off hours and on the weekends. When I got the envelope in the mail and it started out by saying, "We regret to inform," it felt like someone had punched me in the stomach and kicked my dog. My classmates called to console me, but after the initial shock, I realized the reason I didn't pass is because I wasn't prepared the first time. People said things like, "Well, John F. Kennedy Jr. took the exam five times, and many people take it twice." But there was nothing anyone could say to make me feel better. That November day when I opened the first letter after waiting almost six months for the results, I told myself I would be more prepared than any other candidate the second time around.

I studied night and day, for a minimum of ten hours a day, for thirteen weeks straight. *Every day!* It was exhausting and difficult. I did not talk to friends, I barely talked with family, I lived on protein bars and caffeine, and I had a permanent spot at my local library. I actually trained my brain to have photographic recall, like my friend had. I had close to 300 handwritten pages of notes, meticulously organized by subject. I could close my eyes and see my notes, every word. It was remarkable, and I was prepared.

When the time came to sit for the bar exam, I felt that I knew more about the law than any person in that room, including all of the Harvard Law graduates. The exam takes two days, and when you walk into the large room, you see hundreds of people in various states of anxiety, all hoping to be lawyers. The ones you can almost guarantee will not pass are the ones walking in with notes, frantically looking down at them, trying to cram last-minute facts into their brains. I walked in the first day with just my driver's license and my #2 pencils. I knew I was prepared. After the first day, I did not think about the first day's questions or whether I got them right or wrong; I went to the gym, had dinner, watched a little television, and briefly went over the subjects that were going to come up the next day. On day two, I walked in confident, ready to show the Board of Bar Overseers that I was prepared and a worthy candidate to be a member of the bar. Several months later I got the envelope and it told me what I already knew—I passed.

The 3 P's + 1 P helped ensure that I was going to pass. The funny thing is that when you pass the bar exam, you do not know your score; you only receive your score when you don't pass. But, I would be willing to bet that I was in the top 10 percent of the candidates on those two days. Then in June of 2004, I was sworn in at the historic Faneuil Hall in Boston, Massachusetts, and signed my name in the same book as the second president of the United States, John Adams.

KNOW WHAT YOU WANT TO—OR SHOULD I SAY *WILL*—ACHIEVE

Remember the story about my Rolex watch? That was something that I wanted. As I said in the story, my high school buddies had a different set of "wants." Some would consider a Rolex a gluttonous piece of jewelry. However, it was a *goal* I set that I achieved. Is a Rolex something you want? Well, only you can determine that. And what you want is something that you do need to determine.

There are many theories about *goal* setting. There are many ideas about how to properly meet your goals and dreams. Some say you need to set achievable goals, midlevel goals, and stretch goals. Some theories try to dissuade people from setting unrealistic and stretch goals because that only sets people up for failure. I don't agree; that type of thought process in and of itself is negative. If you want something, if you really yearn for something, then focus on it and take *action* to get it. Set your goals as high as you want. If you focus and take *action*, you will achieve your *goal* and get what you want. One very useful technique to keep you focused and remind you of what *you* want is making a dream board: a collage of things you want. The "things" do not have to be material. For instance, if you want happiness, then put the word *happiness* on your dream board. Put on it the house you want, the vacation destination you want, or whatever else your goal is, and look at your dream board every day. I know many successful people who have dream boards— because they work.

I use a very similar technique, but I have pictures of things in my office that I want. I had a picture of a watch that I wanted. It was directly behind my desk so that when I actually walked into my office every day I would see it. About a year ago, I was in a spa at the Del Hotel on Coronado Island, and I opened my locker. Guess what was in the locker? The exact watch I wanted. On June 9, 2012, I actually sent a tweet from @MikeAlden2012 with a picture of the watch. Now, I did not imagine that was how I would acquire the watch, and as you would expect, I gave it to the attendant. But, about a week later I went and tried that watch on. It was a Ulysse Nardin. It turns out I didn't like how it felt on my wrist. I still love the style; it just wasn't a fit. But, I saw another watch I liked and wanted. I tried on this new watch several times, I looked at pictures of it online, and I kept pictures of this watch on my computer screen when I was in my office. Guess what? I just bought that watch about a week ago, and it is very similar in quality to a Ulysse Nardin.

What you and I want may be very different. But what really matters to *you* is not what I want, it is what *you* want. So, I ask you: What do you want, and how are you going to get it?

ARE YOU SMARTER THAN A FIRST-GRADER? THEN YOU CAN SET GOALS

My daughter is in first grade, and we recently worked on her biography. Her teachers assigned things the biography should discuss, such as people they love, where they were born, important events, and other things about their lives. At the end of the assignment the teacher asked that the students discuss their dreams and goals and how they will accomplish them. It was totally amazing to me! First-graders were being taught to *ask* for what they wanted! My daughter is very lucky to be able to go to private school where they are teaching her this kind of thing at such a young age. I asked several people who have kids in first grade in public school, and no such question has been asked.

They asked, *What are your goals and dreams, and what do you need to do to reach your goals and dreams?* I have to say I was totally amazed by this question. From my own childhood, I remember being asked things like, "What do you want to be when you grow up?" But such a very pointed, direct question for seven-year-olds is amazing.

When I was working on the part of the biography we were supposed to help her with, I asked my daughter what her dreams were and then asked what she wanted to be when she grew up. I worked with her closely and we came up with this: "When I grow up I want to be a singer. I will need to practice every day to meet this goal." But incredibly, then my seven-year-old little girl, on her own, changed what we collectively came up with to this: "When I grow up I *will* be a singer. I will need to practice every day to meet *my* goal."

She changed it to take ownership of her dream and goal of being a singer. She *will* be a singer and it is *her* goal. I always try to teach my daughter about goals and dreams and how to be successful—little, subtle things, but I can't take credit for the above. I can attribute it to her teachers or most likely her seven-year-old, uninfected mind. She has not been infected with excusetosis yet, and her DNA has not been modified by negative thoughts. Take it from my daughter and set goals, then *prepare* to achieve your goals and dreams.

Remember Gladwell's common denominator for successful people in *Outliers? Ten thousand hours!* I agree with his findings; however, you don't need this amount of time to change the way you think, change your diet, change your financial future, or change the negative influences in your life. You just need to say that you *will* do it and that it is *your* dream and goal, and then prepare. Ask yourself this: Are you smarter than a first-grader?

BY THE WAY . . . WHAT DID I WANT TO BE?

Just in case you are wondering . . . Yes, when I was in elementary school, they had us write down what we wanted to be when we grew up. Most boys wrote things like doctor, fireman, or policeman. I wrote down lawyer. I am not sure if I knew what a lawyer was back then, but I knew that I didn't like not knowing my rights. For kids growing up in the projects, police can be a good or a bad thing. I remember feeling powerless as a kid when police were in my house. I became a lawyer, not with the idealistic or naïve view of changing the world, but simply to have the education first for myself. Twenty-odd years after writing down what I wanted to be, my reasons stayed the same. It was to build value in me and what I knew. Everything else would fall into place.

LEARNING HOW TO SELL

Most schools across the country and across the world have fundraisers for things such as school supplies and paying for future field trips. My school was no different. I went to public schools until college, and at every level we had to sell something. We sold chocolate bars, candles, magazines, and gifts for the holiday season. I remember being excited about each new selling *opportunity* because we would usually be rewarded for our sales. Many kids' parents just bought the amount of widgets needed so their child could be rewarded. Fortunately, I did not have parents who could do that. I would of course hit up my immediate family, and my mom or dad would sometimes try to bring stuff to work, so collectively they were always good for a few sales, but in order to really win a big prize or be recognized, I had to find my customers.

As early as nine years of age I would canvass the surrounding neighborhoods, selling magazines or chocolate bars to strangers. Yes, I would be alone! Probably not the best idea at any time in history, but that is what I did. I can't say that I remember each interaction, but I can say that my parents' inability to buy my way to a prize gave me the ability to sell. To do so, I was forced to *think* of a way to sell those things and *get* what I wanted.

In retrospect the prizes looked much better in the catalogue than in person. But, I *wanted* the prize and had to *get* it. I used what every single one of us has—my mind and my body—to accomplish my *goal*. I was never the top seller, because most of my customers were parents buying stuff for their kids anyway, but I was always above the average, and most of the time I got the prize I was shooting for. The important thing is that I was learning the skills I needed, learning to *ask* for what I wanted. I was preparing to ask for *more*.

ASK FOR *MORE* THAN WHAT YOU WANT

Regardless of what you decide you want, don't settle for that. This is very important and usually forgotten. A while ago I was discussing with my accountant our cash flow needs. We had a significant amount of money sitting in what we call a reserve account. This reserve account is actually held in trust by my merchant processor. The merchant processor makes the decision about how much money to hold and how much to release back to my company. After a discussion with my accountant, we decided that if we could get $100,000 released back to us and reduce the amount of reserve the merchant processor held in trust that our cash flow that particular week and long-term would be greatly improved. Well, I *asked* my merchant processor for $250,000 and that they stop taking a reserve. Because of my *relationship* with my merchant processor and our history, they gave me what I *asked* for. My accountant was elated. I knew what I wanted, I *asked* for more, and I got it. Too many times, whether it be negotiating for the price of a car or asking for a raise, people leave money on the table. *Ask* for more and you will get *more*. It's not greed, it's getting what you deserve. Ask for more out of yourself and you will *get more*.

TIPS TO GET MORE CHIPS: WHAT YOU NEED TO KNOW BEFORE THE NEGOTIATION

When most people hear the word "negotiation," they feel uneasy or anxious. Nobody in this country likes the activity of negotiation. The fact is, much like the point I made in the beginning of this chapter about buying and selling, everything you do in your life is at some point a negotiation. You negotiate your way through the traffic to work by allowing others to pass at your expense or by passing someone else in order to make it to work on time. You negotiate your way through the crowd at the train station. You may not even say a word, but you and everyone around you has decided to give and take something in order to accomplish a goal. This is not to be confused with navigation, which merely means trying to get from point A to point B. As you navigate your way to work, you negotiate with the others around you. You negotiate with your family members about basic things like TV time, bathroom time, and who gets to use the family car.

You also negotiate with yourself every day. You are fighting the disease of excusetosis and effectively negotiating with yourself by finding ways to get things done. When you wake up you may be tired, but as a part of your treatment for the disease, you tell yourself that you are full of energy and ready to get through the day. As you can see by these examples, it *is* in your genetic makeup to negotiate. You could not survive without negotiation. As you will see in the following, we all do this naturally. Once you understand that negotiation is a part of your human instincts, negotiation no longer becomes negotiation. It becomes a subconscious involuntary response to a situation in which you are trying to get more, and you deserve it.

So for the rest of this chapter I will share with you some important realizations that will prepare you to negotiate like a pro. Once you get these in your head, they will transform you from someone who settles for less to someone who is prepared to ask for more.

NEGOTIATE LIKE A FIVE-YEAR-OLD: WHY ASK WHY? . . . WHY NOT?

When my daughter Morgan was five years old, she used to ask "why" all the time. Now, most child psychologists might explain this by saying that this age is the most impressionable age, and that the brain of a five-year-old is growing rapidly and also absorbing information both consciously and subconsciously. If you have kids, I am sure you have noticed how the typical five-year-old would ask you "why" any time you say "no." They ask "why" with no inhibitions; they are unapologetic, and they just keep asking, "Why? Why can't I have M&Ms for breakfast? Why can't I have that stuffed animal that is so cute and cuddly? Why do I have to brush my teeth? Why do I have to go to bed? Why can't I stay up for one more show?" You get the picture. Many times a new parent has no idea what to say to these "whys." The standard response is, "Because I said so."

Now, my daughter may not really be negotiating with me—or is she? Where did she learn to ask "why" at five years old? I have to honestly say, despite my wife's and my stellar parenting skills, she didn't learn to ask "why" from us. Maybe she learned it from SpongeBob, but the reality is she doesn't know anything else. It is in our genetic makeup to negotiate. But, somewhere along the line, we suppress the instinctive trait of negotiating.

Now, asking "why" as a five-year-old isn't always negotiating, because it may be part of their cognitive growth and development, as those psychologists say. As in, "Why did the cat die?" or, "Why is the sky blue?" (good luck answering those). But my daughter's sub-conscious mind definitely contains the innate skill and behavior that has been with us since the beginning of mankind. Cavemen negoti-ated with each other about who would get what food and territory. As we evolved, the negotiation skill became more cerebral and involved less violence—except for war, which is the ultimate negotiation. Up until society suppresses the negotiation gene, the question "why?" is a very effective negotiating question, and at the end of the day, nego-tiation is a part of our genetic survival makeup, one that we can use to get valuable information that will help us to negotiate for more. Take for instance the following:

› Why won't you sell it for less?

› Why can't you discount the price?

› Why is the price so high when your competitors sell the same product for less?

› Why can't you honor a competitor's coupon?

› Why won't you throw in a few extra if I buy twelve?

During the heat of any negotiation, the five-year-old's question of "why" is very powerful, as it disarms the other person and forces him or her to think. While they are thinking, most people will take the path of least resistance: "Well, if you buy twelve, I will throw in a few extra." "We don't normally honor a competitor's coupon, but I will today." Some people make up the answer, such as "Sorry, they don't let us discount." That is—pardon my French—BS. Just recently I bought four brand new suits at a high-end clothing store, the type of clothing store that offers you champagne or espresso when you are shopping. This was the second time I was there and the second purchase I made. My first purchase was a blazer and a few shirts. I used the phrase that you will learn in the next chapter, and the clerk said she couldn't, and she didn't discount my purchase. Why do I tell you about this temporary defeat? Well, with my second purchase I asked again, and this time she found the owner, who gave me a significant discount, gave me his personal cell phone number, and thanked me himself. In later chapters we discuss more on how to use the skills developed and mastered by a five-year-old.

WHY ASK WHY? Because it works!

WHAT ARE THEY THINKING?

When you are in a negotiation, you need to determine what the other person has and what they want. My 3 P's + 1 P technique will help answer these questions. For instance, if you are purchasing a car, you *need* to know what the invoice is on the car, what incentives are being offered, and what other dealerships are selling the car for. If you know what the other party wants and what they have, then before you even say a word you will be in a very powerful negotiating position.

WHAT ARE YOU THINKING?

You need to know what you want, and what you have as well. You see, the other person, especially in a retail setting, is already sizing you up, and they probably already know how to get what they want out of you. So you need to know what you want out of *you* as well. This goes back to what I was saying in the beginning of the chapter: know what you want; it's important. In a car purchase scenario (more about this in the next chapter), you need to know what your bottom line is and what kind of car you want. If you walk into a dealership "just to look," then you are not ready to negotiate.

When you are ready, be on high alert, as buying a car, like many purchases, is an emotional experience. Buying anything on emotion is almost always a losing situation for you. So know what you want. People say, "Don't go grocery shopping on an empty stomach, because if you do, you will end up buying things that you don't need." You also end up spending your hard-earned money on junk. Just like the grocery store, don't ever enter any negotiation situation without knowing what you want and what the other party wants.

WIN-WIN NEGOTIATING

Too many people negotiate with the winner-take-all mentality and are more concerned with "winning" and destroying the other party. I am not a fan of this technique—it usually doesn't work and it frequently ruins the relationship with the other party. Now, you may say, "Well, who cares if I offend a clerk at Macy's or a car salesperson?" I have often had situations where I had to deal with businesspeople I did not like. However, I negotiated with them in good faith and in a way that allowed both of us to win, and guess what? I continue to do business with them. By knowing what the other party is thinking and what they have, you are able to negotiate a deal that allows them to make a living while getting yourself the best deal. You will be surprised how the same tactics you use with the Macy's clerk can also be used in major business deals that can net you millions. This may be difficult to grasp, but when you realize that winning the battle does not always win the war, you will find this technique will pay off in the long run.

LOOKING DOWN

In 1989, a young black man humbly shined people's shoes every day to make ends meet. He was reported to always be happy and appreciative. Many people looked down on him as though he were nothing more than just a shoe shiner.

But this young black man was also an aspiring stand-up comedian who worked clubs at night and shined shoes by day. Fast-forward to

2004, and that young man is one of the most recognized and powerful entertainers in the world, a musician, comedian, and acclaimed actor. That man, Eric Marlon Bishop, also known as Jamie Foxx, accepted the Oscar for his portrayal of Ray Charles in the movie *Ray*. You would probably never guess that the man shining your shoes today could be the next big thing tomorrow, so be nice to people when you negotiate.

DEFERRING TO A THIRD PARTY

This is a great technique when buying, selling, or in any negotiation, especially when it is impromptu. The typical scenario goes like this: You are interested in buying something and you begin to discuss the purchase with the salesperson. You don't feel comfortable with the price or even the salesperson. The easiest way to get out of the situation is by saying, "I need to discuss this with my wife/spouse/ brother/sister/grandmother." The person you mention doesn't matter. Let's assume you are not comfortable with the price, and because of that you decide to use this technique. The salesperson can then do a number of things. We discuss this technique in a later chapter from the salesperson's perspective, but this simple technique can be used to get you more out of any situation.

BE PREPARED TO WALK AWAY

When you enter into a negotiation, you need to be prepared to walk away from the deal. This takes discipline and sometimes a little drama, but in any negotiation you need to be prepared to walk away. If for some reason none of the techniques we discuss in this book are effective in your negotiation, be prepared to walk away. I don't care if it is your dream home, dream car, or a chocolate truffle, be prepared to walk away if you do not get the deal you know you can get. Many people walk away from deals to avoid confrontation as a result of their inability to control their emotions. When you use my 3 P's + 1 P technique and you know what they want and what you want, then walking away is just another tactic, not a knee-jerk, emotional reaction. Walking away from a deal is a powerful and sometimes risky maneuver, but nine times out of ten it gets you a better deal.

People often send me products that they want my company to market, and there was one product in particular that I fell in love with—it was unique and had mass appeal. In addition, it was already developed and was a great all-around product. The inventor is a nice guy, but he didn't understand my business and wanted a very large royalty. Financially, his request didn't make sense for my company. Now, I can't stress how much I loved this product. We went back and forth several times, and it appeared we were not able to come to a deal, so I walked away. I didn't get emotional, even though I must admit I was frustrated, but I was prepared to walk away if the deal was not a win-win agreement. Several months later, the owner reached out to me and agreed to the terms I proposed. As I type this page, we are in negotiations with another multinational company that is going to do a joint venture with my firm. This deal will most likely generate tens of millions of dollars.

The key points to remember in any negotiation strategy are:

› Being prepared is important.

› Understand what your goal is during the negotiation.

› Have as much knowledge as possible.

› Be prepared to walk away.

› Take the deal when you have achieved your pre-set goal.

TAKE THE DEAL

I have witnessed large business negotiations collapse not only due to a lack of preparedness, but also because of greed and not really knowing what was wanted. When you know the purpose of your negotiation strategy and you achieve your goal, then be prepared to take the deal. It may seem hypocritical to say such a thing for a book titled *Ask More, Get More,* but you will learn you can still ask more and get more without losing the deal.

Taking the deal that you have in front of you takes discipline. Successful professional gamblers who earn a living playing cards or table games set a daily limit or a goal *up* or *down.* If their goal is to make $1,000 and they hit that goal—they walk away. If their threshold for a loss is also $1,000—they also walk away. Successful professional gamblers take the deal that is beneficial to them. By the way, there are not too many professional gamblers. They are an elite group of people who are very prepared and disciplined and who are constantly studying and exercising ways to control their breathing and thoughts. But at the end of the day, *they take the deal*. When a professional gambler walks into a casino, the house doesn't have a chance—that is why many pros are banned from the casino.

USE TECHNOLOGY TO YOUR ADVANTAGE

I am a big fan of the telephone, and I use the telephone for almost 90 percent of the deals that I put together. Maybe it's because I have a large call center or perhaps because my grandfather had call centers in the '50s. But I actually think it is because of the ease with which we can instantly communicate with people all over the world. Some people prefer to look into the whites of another's eyes. As for me, I can tell if the individual is a good person just by what they say and how they say it. If you are going to make a big transaction buying or selling something, use the phone as a way to gather information as a part of your preparation. Ask as many questions as you feel necessary; this will prepare you if you need to come face-to-face.

INTERNET

Today we can google everything. The Internet is so powerful that you can find almost anything you want, but you must check your sources. Many websites seem to have accurate information, but in reality are not even close. After you find the information you think you need, become a detective and check your sources.

EMAIL

I have a 250-page book somewhere in my library that teaches people how to communicate properly via email. There is a definite value in knowing how to communicate this way. What I usually do in a negotiation being conducted through email is write the message, save the draft, and review it—before I send it. I think about how the other person could react when they read my words, and I ask myself, "Does the email effectively communicate what I want?" I spell-check one more time, reread, and then I hit "send."

CHAPTER 6

HOW TO NEGOTIATE FOR MORE: THE PHRASE THAT WILL MAKE YOU MORE MONEY, SAVE YOU MORE MONEY, AND INCREASE YOUR BOTTOM LINE—GUARANTEED!

"IS THERE ANYTHING ELSE YOU CAN DO FOR ME?"

That is the phrase. Think about it: "Is there anything else you can do for me?" What is the phrase really asking? Well, it depends on your situation. I use this in virtually every aspect of my life, from negotiation with business associates to taking my car in for repairs to buying a Diet Coke at McDonald's.

Let's say you are trying to get a discount on a service bill at your dealership that is unexpectedly high. When you walk into the car dealership, a service technician, who by the way is a highly trained and skilled salesperson, greets you. In this scenario, the service technician, who, again I stress, is "trained" to "help you," has an ulterior motive that affects his personal compensation. When you are presented with the cost of the service bill, the technician will "help you out" by mentioning all the work that "must" be done on your car. The technician will explain that your car needs tires and new filters, and that you need these to operate the vehicle at optimal and safe levels. Many times—if not every time—the customer agrees to the price, or maybe says things like, "Wow, that is high," or "I didn't expect that," or "That's too expensive." These statements are defensive in nature and offensive to the highly skilled service technician, causing him to be less likely to "help you."

When presented with the bill, rather than getting excited and agitated, ask the service technicians the magic question: "Is there anything else you can do for me?" In their mind they are thinking many things like, "What does he mean?" "Is he looking for a discount?" "Is he looking for a free detail?" The beauty is, that is up to you. In most instances the service technician will sharpen his pencil and give you a reduced price. How can I say this with confidence? Because I do it every time I bring my car in for service, and I save money each time. Additionally, many of my friends, family members, and employees have done this exact thing and saved hundreds of dollars off of their service bills.

Now, it doesn't stop there. If your goal is to get a reduced price, then *great*, you just saved money. Let's say you saved $50—for many people that is a half-day of pay—and the true cost of your ownership of your car has been reduced by $50. Now multiply that by four on an annual basis—four being the average number of times someone brings a car in for service. You pocketed $200, which is like making $57,000 if invested in the stock market with an average rate of return of 12 percent for fifty years. Cut the years in half, and $200 saved is still $23,500! This number is not exact due to compound interest, but you get the picture.

But why stop there? Next comes a follow-up question, all within the premise of the service technician helping you: "*What else* can you do for me?" When asking a follow-up question, it is paramount that you ask this question with absolute sincerity. What you are really saying is, "Are you really going to charge me that much, make me go somewhere else, get it cheaper, and ultimately become an unhappy customer? Does that make you feel good?" He is also thinking, "Well, did he get a price somewhere else? Has he had this done here before?"

IT'S ALL RIGHT FOR THEM TO ASK—AND FOR YOU TO ASK, TOO!

There is nothing wrong with the service technician trying to make money, as we live in a capitalist society and that is one thing that makes this country great. But, there is equally *nothing wrong* with making your hard-earned dollar stretch and make you money.

People sometimes may get embarrassed by *asking* for more. Some people may consider it cheap or even rude. I am a very generous person, but there is nothing cheap about me when I ask for more. Having the benefit of being around ultra-wealthy people, one thing I noticed was that the rich do not worry about being cheap, and sometimes others think they are being rude. But, in all reality they are doing what got them to where they are, *asking* for more. Ask yourself: Would you rather have your money, or give it to someone else? As I mentioned earlier, people in countries all around the world negotiate and bargain all day long in a very open and outgoing manner. Some in the United States may find it comical or even rude; well, erase that thought from your mind if you believe it. Asking for more means more for you, more for your favorite charity, more for your family, and more out of life.

The follow-up question may save you more money at that very moment, but it may also save you money down the line. The service technician who knows that you are funding his paycheck wants you to come back. So, he may give you a coupon for the next trip or offer to have your car detailed. Either way, it is a win-win scenario, as discussed earlier in the book. You got your car serviced for less—and maybe get a free detail or coupon—and the service technician "sold you" on the service and retained a customer.

THAT LITTLE QUESTION WILL TAKE YOU A LONG WAY

I was speaking with a friend of mine who is the ultimate pessimist. My friend kept going on about how this technique wouldn't work because of this or that, and I said, "Try it next time you *purchase* or *pay*"—there is difference—"for anything." He had some old gold jewelry that he wanted to sell for scrap. He brought the jewelry in, and they told him they would give him $150 for it. My friend proudly told me he then asked, "Is there anything else you can do for me?" and said nothing else. The man behind the counter looked at the gold and his calculator and said, "Yeah, I can give you $175." Doesn't seem like much, but $25 will put gas in your tank, fill your belly, or add up to thousands of dollars in your retirement account.

Thousands of dollars? Yeah, thousands! Let's say the above real story happened in 1980. Now let's assume you put that meager $25 into a retirement account and your average rate of return was 12 percent annually; you would have $7,225 in fifty years. You need to change the way you see things. That meager $25 today is really $7,225 over a fifty-year time span. It's not just twenty-five bucks—it's your future!

You may be wondering why I bother telling you a story about $25. I tell it because it is a real story, and you can start using this phrase immediately. Most important, it's also scalable. What do I mean by scalable? Well, you can increase or even decrease the amounts to figure out how much *richer* or how much closer you are to becoming truly financially free if you begin using this phrase over time. If you can apply this single phrase to your daily routine and habits, you will *make* thousands of dollars a year. For some, it may be tens of thousands, and at higher levels it can become *millions.* I have used the phrase and made *millions* of dollars during the worst economic slump in the history of the United States, if not the world. The dealership scenario was a true story that happened to me personally, and I saved $200. I can easily invest this $200 and turn it into $57,000 through programs that are available to anyone.

If you are reading this book and you are a multimillionaire, you may feel like you don't need to "save" $25. You need to reset that type of thinking. If you are reading this book and it was difficult for you to come up with the money to pay for it, you may be thinking the same thing. My response is the same: There is an address at the back of this book. Feel free to send me $25, and if you do, I will make the check out to the United Way. Saving $25 now is really making *thousands of dollars.*

ARE YOU A BELIEVER YET? YOU NEED TO BE!

There is another thing I want to point out about the above story—my friend is a pessimist about everything. He most likely only half-believed the phrase would work. When your belief level is higher and you truly believe that the techniques in this book will work, your success rate will be much higher. *You must believe* in what you are doing. We, as human beings, can sense and tell when another is not confident in his or her actions. Ever hear the phrase, "they can smell your fear"? Most animals can actually smell when you are afraid and can be more aggressive with you. Humans can also sense when you are not confident in your actions. When your confidence level is low, you are less likely to achieve your goals. You must, in your core, believe that the techniques in this book will work. Imagine if my friend's confidence level was higher when he used the phrase; maybe he would have gotten more.

THE DIFFERENCE BETWEEN PAYING AND PURCHASING

Earlier I said there is a difference between paying for and purchasing something. We *pay* for things we need, like food, clothes, gas, and electricity . . . you know, the basic things that we need to live in a normal society. I believe you *purchase* things that are not necessary to live in a modern society, like a car, a computer, your cable, or your Internet service.

Why do I differentiate between the two? Well, when most people *pay* for things, they accept the price without thinking. They get a bill and they *pay* it, month after month, without thinking. What if next time you get a bill that you have to *pay*, you use the phrase? What if it saved you 20 percent off your home energy bill? That would be worth the cost of the book, right? Of course it would. Did you know the average yearly cost for home energy *pay*out is $240 *billion* in the Unites States? Could you use an extra $48 billion? That's 20 percent of $240 billion. The number seems too large to grasp, but on an individual level that equates to roughly $420 a year. If you ask my question for things that you *pay* for, you will save and *make* thousands of dollars a year. But, like the lottery, you can't win if you don't play. If you don't ask the question, you will never know the answer. Most of us are willing to "save" money off of things we *purchase*, and as a society, we *purchase* a lot of things, but it's important to remember to use my phrase when you *pay* for things, also.

WHY IT ALWAYS WORKS!

Did you notice something about the gold scenario? It wasn't a *purchase* or a *buy*, it was a *sale*. Yeah, the phrase works in that scenario, too. You see, it is my belief that as human beings we are inherently creatures who want to help each other. If I were wrong, then the world wouldn't exist. Everyone needs help, and everyone likes to give help and feel good about it. That is why I use the phrase, "Is there anything else you can do for me?" You see, I am essentially asking for help, and humans instinctively help each other. So the phrase, even with the most highly skilled and hardened people, triggers something in their brains. In many instances without even realizing it, many people subconsciously "help" you. This phrase breaks down all the barriers that are up in a *pay, sell*, or *purchase* situation, and the person on the other end of the question subconsciously and briefly forgets about personal pecuniary interests.

I was on the phone—a cell phone (one device that seems to have morphed from a *purchase* to a *pay* item)—a few weeks back with a friend of mine about this book and the phrase. He was telling me how he was waiting for a call back from his telecom company, because he thought the current rate they were charging him was too high. He was going to tell them that he was going to switch to another carrier. As I alluded to earlier, before you ask the phrase, you have to ask yourself, "What is your goal? What do you want?" I asked my friend what he wanted. I asked him several questions: "Do you like your phone? Do you get good reception? Is the price similar to that of other carriers?" He said he just wants to lower his bill, as he was only upset about the cost. I told him to relax, and when he speaks with the carrier—most likely a person with limited authority—explain that he likes the service and the phone and has been a customer for several years, but feels the monthly fee was high, and that he wondered if "there was anything they could do for him?"

You see, this is a modification (like "*What* else can you do for me?") of the phrase (there was no "else"), but it accomplishes the same thing. It magically broke down the tense situation into one in which the other person was now trying to help my friend. The other person had a job to do, and that job ultimately was to use the limited power that the representative had in order to keep a satisfied customer. My friend got his phone bill reduced by several hundred dollars over the life of his agreement. As we mentioned earlier, before you use this powerful phrase, ask yourself what the other person wants to accomplish, and know what you want to accomplish. In this scenario, we were dealing with a customer service agent who had limited power. Because this person was now "helping" my friend, she found a way to save and make him *hundreds of dollars.*

Just today my friend who sold the gold came to me and said he used the technique. He caught me off guard, and I didn't understand what he meant. So, he said it again: "I *used the technique!*" He told me how he saved $40 a month off his cable bill, got more channels, and received $300 in gift cards by saying one simple thing: "Is there anything else you can do for me?" He is now a believer!

This one phrase will change your life! Also know that saving $480 ($40 per month times twelve months) is like making more than $100,000 over fifty years. Think about it: Saving $480 is like *making* $100,000! Could you use an extra $100,000 when you retire?

Another friend named John recently came to me to tell me an amazing story about totaling his car. He was on the highway, hit a slick part of the road, did a 360, hit the guardrail, and ultimately totaled his car. Since he wasn't hurt in the accident, I asked if anyone else was injured, and he said no. I said, "Thank God," and I thought that was the end of his story.

John then told me that he bought his car for $8,900 a year ago, and the insurance company told him they were willing to give him $7,300 for his car. John told me that when he asked one question, "Is there anything else you can do for me?" the insurance agent responded by asking, "What were you thinking?"

Now, this part is important. John knew in his head what he wanted before asking the all-important phrase that pays. He wanted $8,000, so he told her he was thinking in the $8,300 range. John was assuming they would meet at $8,000; to his surprise—because, as he admitted to me, he had not fully bought into my techniques— she agreed to $8,000. By asking this one simple question, John made $700, and it is *tax free*! But, John proudly told me, he wasn't done. After she agreed, he said, "Well, is there *any more* you can do for me?" John asked this because at the time of the accident, he happened to have a flat-screen TV in his car. As you can expect, the TV was ruined. She asked him how much the TV was worth, and he told her $250. She said, "Sure, that is a part of your insurance and we will cut you a check for an additional $250." John had now *made* close to $1,000 tax-free just by asking. But he still wasn't done: he then told the agent how he had to pay out-of-pocket tow fees because AAA didn't cover towing on the highway. Guess what? He got compensated for that, too.

This is a great story. It shows that the technique works, but what it also proves is that this works in every situation. Most people would just accept the amount the insurance company was offering. But not John: he knew about my technique, and it made him $1,000! Don't accept the first offer, and don't assume the technique won't work with big companies.

They work!

They work!

They work!

A DOLLAR SAVED IS A DOLLAR ASKED FOR: BRIEF TESTIMONIALS

So here are just a few of the victories people I know have had using my technique—just some random samples of people I asked in passing while writing the book. And now that the secret is out, there are bound to be thousands more across America!

› Saved $15 on a shipping charge for some hard drives—Mike S.
› Saved $30 on shipping for lost credit card and got card sent overnight—Tim C.

> Got two premium channels for cable television for free, a $40 value—Mike S.

> Saved $10 on a lunch, by asking if they could reduce the bill —Ryan

> Saved $13 on printing costs for a project—Shauna F.

> Saved $100 on a membership charge for the Chamber of Commerce—John M.

> Saved 10 percent on chiropractic work for an entire year—Chris M.

> Saved $4,000 on a home HVAC system—Andrew M.

> Saved $4,000 on dental work *and* got two more teeth done— Mike P.

> Saved $100 on a christening banquet charge—Andrew M.

> Reduced debt by $360 by asking credit card company to reduce the bill—Andrew M.

> Saved $25 on service bill at Land Rover—Kristin S.

> Saved my company $500,000 by asking a finance company to reduce their rate—Jason B.

> Got my company an extra $100,000 by asking American Express to increase our line of credit—Jeff J.

> Saved $23,000 on a Porsche engine by *asking* Porche headquarters if there was anything they could do for me, even though my Porche was out of warranty—Matt R.

A FEW MORE MAGIC QUESTIONS TO NEGOTIATE FOR MORE

Many people don't ask any questions. When you get a bill, do you ask yourself, "Is this right?" Or do you ask the representative if there is any way they could reduce the amount? To some people, asking for a discount after you get the bill is unethical. But, there is *nothing* wrong with making sure the bill is accurate or asking for a discount off the current bill. Most companies will do it, and it is a very effective negotiation tool.

But here are some other great questions that work magically in reducing what you have to take out of your pocket:

"CAN WE ACCOMPLISH THE SAME THING FOR LESS MONEY?"

This question will prompt the seller to think if they can reduce the price or maybe give you something else of value. I used this question when I had my bathroom redone, and saved $1,000. How did this happen? The contractor just spent an extra day in the bathroom himself, rather than having a crew in there. My bathroom was done a day later, but I saved $1,000! *Just by asking!* Just recently, when purchasing some media for one of our products, I used this exact phrase as a follow-up to, "Is there anything else you can do for me?" I wound up saving a total of $5,000, and I got *twice* the number of impressions I was looking for.

"IS THAT THE BEST YOU CAN DO?"

This is a very commonly used question and the answer is almost always "Yes, that is the best I can do." In response to their answer, ask it again. "Is that the best you can do? Really?" This is a very effective technique and will save you money almost every time. This phrase is effective, because most people have heard it or encountered it at one time or another in their lives. As a result, this familiar phrase almost always gets a follow-up, which is usually even more effective if the person *asking* doesn't get what they want. I was in sales training and the trainer said it takes five *no*'s before you get a *yes*; sometimes the follow-up is where you *get* what you want.

"DO YOU HAVE ANY DISCOUNTS AVAILABLE?"

I have my work clothes dry-cleaned at a local dry cleaner, and I have been going there for a few years. One day, I asked, "Do you have any discounts available?" The answer was yes, and for three years I've received a 15 percent discount on my dry cleaning. This discount has saved me hundreds of dollars a year. This question is a great one to use in *big box* retailers. I use it at places like Macy's, Bloomingdale's, Best Buy, Walmart, and Target, and I save money every time! I could fill pages with examples from people who tell me this works. *It does!*

"I MADE A MISTAKE; WHAT CAN YOU DO FOR ME?"

We all make mistakes, and I make them every day. Recognizing that you made the mistake is extremely important. Many people, even after recognizing that they made a mistake, do not realize that you can fix it by using not only the phrase, "What else can you do for me?" but also the other strategies and techniques in this book.

Recently, a friend of mine made a mistake when leasing a new car. He went from his 2010 car to a new 2011 in late December of 2011. The mistake he made was that he paid his lease payment in December for his old car and then got his new car without realizing his December payment was for the use of his old car in January 2012. He caught his mistake a few months later and called the dealership to explain. Calling a car dealership and asking them to write you a check is a very formidable task. My friend calmly explained how the mistake was made and asked if there was anything they could do for him. Sure enough, they obliged by giving him a $500 credit in the service department. So you see, the techniques in this book for negotiating for more can be used even after a negotiation has happened. Don't let pride get in the way of your financial future.

BELIEVE MORE!

As I type, one of my employees entered my office to tell me he used the "technique" on his credit card company. My employee explained that he had accumulated 90,000 points on his credit card that he was anticipating using for *free* travel, but the points expired. He called his credit card company and explained the situation. Then he asked, "Is there anything you can do for me?" They said, "Yes, we will credit you back half of the points today." He followed up with a sincere thank-you and then asked, "What about tomorrow? Can you give me back all of the points tomorrow?" The person on the telephone chuckled and said, "I have never had anyone ask that question, but yes, I will." My employee made an honest mistake and just wanted it to be rectified, and by asking questions he got what he wanted. Ask *more*, and you will *get more*.

WHAT DO SALESPEOPLE KNOW, AND HOW DO I KNOW WHEN I AM BEING SOLD?

I learned so much of the material above from being an insider in the sales world, since I am a salesperson. And at the end of the day, knowing what the salesperson knows goes a long way to help you negotiate for more. Now, the market is flooded with thousands of sales training books, and there are hundreds of training courses that legions of salespeople—and wannabe salespeople—flock to every year to hone sales skills they can use against you to sell you stuff. Now there is nothing wrong with learning your craft and perfecting it. A plumber or a machinist learns a certain set of skills and over time perfects and hones those skills to make them better. Salespeople are not bad people, and like any other professional, they hone their skills too. Now clearly there are some bad apples in the sales game. And unfortunately for salespeople, the bad apples seem to get all the attention and hurt the image of the sales profession as a whole.

But more commonly, consumers are often unable to identify the techniques a salesperson is using and thus are ill-equipped to combat them. This lack of preparedness leads to frustration on the part of the consumer and often gives salespeople a bad name. I know I'm painting with a broad brush, but generally, when people are taken advantage of it is usually because they didn't follow the 3 P's + 1 P technique. They then tell their friends about their bad experience, and the salesperson is demonized.

When I was first introduced to selling cars, I had the same perception that most people have—car salespeople are the bottom of the barrel; they are dishonest and intent on screwing people. Well, if that was my perception, why would I take a chance and be employed as a car salesperson? To be honest . . . I saw an advertisement in the newspaper that guaranteed $425 a week, and I needed money. I was fresh out of college and didn't have my life plan mapped out. I was nervous, because I had never sold anything before—at least I didn't think I had.

Both the formal and on-the-job training I received from Ford-Lincoln-Mercury was top-notch. During my first two weeks, all I did was train. The first thing a good salesperson is taught is product knowledge. So, I was determined to know everything about every make and model, and to be successful, I had to. I sat at a desk in the back of the showroom and no one talked to me. Now, this was in 1997 at the height of an economic boom, and people were buying cars just because they could. I felt uneasy and didn't understand why no one talked to me. Finally, when people began to talk to me, it was to tell me that I wasn't cut out for this line of work. I was a "college boy" and this was for men. It shocked me how mean some of the salespeople were to me, but I later learned that I was perceived as someone who was taking money out of their pockets and food off their tables. Eventually, I proved that I was worthy and that I was sticking around. I became friendly with all of the other sales professionals and have maintained relationships with many of them over the years.

Now, I went through this extensive sales training and have supplemented that with all kinds of sales education through the years, because, as I stated earlier, I am a salesperson. But you are a salesperson too, although you may not know it yet. And here is some quick insider information that can transform you from a victim to a player in the sales game.

INSIDER SALES TECHNIQUE: LOWERING CUSTOMER EXPECTATIONS

Often we hear how a particular business is cutthroat, and car selling is one of those businesses. It is not for the faint of heart or for people who are easily offended. One of the on-the-job skills that I learned—and all salespeople learn sooner or later—is to develop tough, thick skin. I had to let things that seemed offensive or rude roll off my back. Salespeople are taught not to be shaken or intimidated. When I first started actually selling cars, we used a technique called "dollar drops." The typical question a customer asked when negotiating was, "Can you reduce the price?" We, as salespeople, were taught to look and act shocked. Then we were supposed to give in and reduce the price—by one dollar. Now imagine—a customer comes in to buy a Grand Marquis for $19,999 and wants a discount. We were taught to say, "Well, if I could get you $19,998, would you buy it right now?" This technique, called "dollar drops," blew up if not done properly, and for a young salesperson it was tough to do. The purpose of this was to lower the expectation of the buyer, while at the same time not offending him or her. After we used this technique, the customer realized that we weren't going to drop the price by thousands. We had effectively lowered their expectations and put the entire sale process into perspective.

INSIDER SALES TECHNIQUE: BUILD RAPPORT AND TAKE CONTROL

When you are not in control of a negotiation, you are more likely to leave money on the table and not get the deal you could have. A good salesperson will first build a rapport with you, usually by asking you questions about your life and what you do. They do this to take your mind off the real reason why you are there. Top-notch salespeople can relate to pretty much any person and are thus perceived as good guys or gals. By building a rapport with you, they now seem more like your friend, and friends always look out for each other, right? When you are asked questions like, "How about them Red Sox?" or "How's the weather?" they are just softening you up and ultimately gaining your trust. Before you know it, they have taken control of the situation and you have no idea what hit you.

It is okay to build rapport. It's also okay as a buyer to interact, but don't let your guard down.

Recently, I got a call from a young man named Rick from my dealership (I drive a Lexus and I mostly lease my vehicles). Rick said something like, "Mike, you are a preferred customer and your current Lexus is in pristine shape. Our inventory is low on your model; if I could get you in a new one for the same price or less, that would be a good deal, right?" Now, the "right?" part is what we call a "tie down," as he asked me a question that pretty much the only rational answer to is "*yes.*" The other leap he took right in the very beginning was addressing me by my first name and not my surname; this makes the sale more personal and less formal, even though we are dealing with a very expensive proposition. This doesn't work in every situation, but it worked with me. So I told him, "Great job on the tie down; I will be there later." It was obvious to me he was well trained. Rick then tried to get me to commit by taking control. He tried to set a time; I responded by saying I would be there when I'd be there. He was nice and friendly, using great tonalities. He had the ability to use his voice to emphasize certain words and was genuinely excited. Rick's excitable and effervescent sales pitch was the key to him closing me. He used his tonalities and the persuasive techniques like rapport building to get me in the door.

During the call I began to use rapport building on him. I asked him where he was from, how long he had been in the business, and told him he was doing a great job. I was doing this so he would both "like me" and really like me. A salesperson will always act as if they like a prospective customer, because it means dollars and cents in his or her pocket. But, if the salesperson genuinely likes you, you are more apt to get a better deal. So, when you are in a situation that involves buying or selling certain items, take an interest in the other person. Whether you are the buyer or the seller, tell them they are doing a great job and ask them questions like "How long have you been doing this?" "Where are you from?" and—one of my favorites when it comes down to making a decision—"Would you do it if you were me?" That question reaches into the moral core of everyone asked, and unless you're dealing with a sociopathic narcissist (e.g., Bernie Madoff), you will get an honest answer.

When I arrived at the dealership, the general manager greeted me, then quickly handed me off to a seasoned car guy named Gene. I told them about the call and picked out a vehicle that I would consider. You see, for me it was initially an offer I couldn't refuse—get a new vehicle at the same price and color I wanted. Gene began to ask all about me, what I did, where I was from, and so forth. I could tell immediately that he was a very nice guy. He was well dressed, well spoken, and likeable. He was very easy to talk to, and made buying or leasing painless. I sat there while they ran the numbers. And I did pick out a car that was slightly more expensive than my original, so I knew they would hit me with a higher payment. I then applied a combination of all of the skills mentioned in this book. One of the easiest to use and most important skills was rapport building with Gene by finding a commonality with him; I sold cars right out of college, so we chatted about the business, and he respected my knowledge. Secondly I used the phrase that pays: "What else can you do for me?" Funny, when I used the phrase, both Gene and Willy (the general manager) were perplexed with the question; their initial response was to claim they couldn't go any lower.

In the end, I got a car with more options than my previous vehicle for roughly $7,000 off the retail price, complete with all-weather mats and leather protection (I have a little girl, so the protection is definitely necessary). In addition, I also got two full tanks of gas—all for virtually the same price as my other car.

How do I know I got a good deal? Well, I followed the 3 P's + 1 P strategy: I had a plan, I knew what they wanted, and I knew what I wanted. Plus, I was prepared to walk away. Could I have negotiated a "better deal"? Maybe it was possible, but highly unlikely. When you are trying to get the best deal possible, all you have to do is implement the strategies and the techniques in this book, and you will never have to ask yourself, "Did I get a good deal?" As I stated earlier, even if you find that you made a mistake, you can still apply the techniques in this book after the fact to minimize the severity of the mistake. You just have to ask!

CHAPTER 7

HOW TO SAVE MORE!

FIRST OF ALL—DON'T BUY WHAT YOU CAN'T AFFORD

A few years ago, *Saturday Night Live* with Steve Martin aired a really funny spoof about the infomercial business. They were mocking a well-known pitchman who has pitched everything from how to get "Free Money" to a tape that cures pain to books that give you a photographic memory. The skit was about a book on how to get out of debt titled *Don't Buy Stuff You Cannot Afford*. It sounds simplistically humorous, but it's also very true. In this *MTV Cribs* society, we want to appear wealthy and seem to be addicted to appearing to have stuff. Remember MC Hammer, a famous rapper who appeared to have everything but lost it all? Or celebrities like Nicolas Cage and others who end up bankrupt or sell off assets simply because they bought things they couldn't afford?

One of the main reasons why the real estate market is a total mess is because too many people bought unaffordable houses. They signed up for exotic mortgages without having to document their income, hoping somehow they could pay for it. The American Dream is to own a home with a white picket fence, but in reality the dream is not realized overnight. As with most things that happen overnight, you eventually wake up in a real nightmare.

I knew a guy who lacked formal education and had no marketable skills, but he got lucky with a get-rich-quick scheme. He went from zero income to making a projected $200,000 a year. However, he was only pacing $200,000 a year, and hadn't yet actually earned that amount over a full year. Despite this, he decided he was going to buy a big home, and I remember thinking, "He is going to lose this house, and his wife and daughter are going to be devastated." Sure enough, less than a year later the get-rich money dried up, and he had no marketable skills to fall back on. Not surprisingly, he couldn't come close to paying his $5,000-a-month mortgage. The bank foreclosed, he lost his home, and he is now living in his in-laws' basement. This is happening all over America, and everyone wants to blame the big banks or financial institutions for creating this chaotic, unstable financial world. In reality, if people only bought things they could afford, we would not be in this crisis.

When you want to buy anything—from a pen to a piece of clothing to a house—ask yourself:

Can I afford to pay for it right now?

Can I afford to part with the cash that I have to get the thing I want?

Do I have a plan to be able to make the monthly mortgage payments, plus all of the other expenses?

If you are not one hundred percent positive, then you can't afford it. It's that simple. If you can't afford it, then you can't buy it. *Period!* Later, I will teach you how to be more disciplined as you run YOU Enterprises, Inc. In the future, with proper planning, you will absolutely get everything you want and desire, but if you are dishonest with yourself, your debt will continue to climb and make financial freedom more difficult.

CASH IS KING

Over the past four decades, the proliferation of credit cards has been extraordinary. In fact, many people only use "plastic." If you are in debt and you want to reduce that debt, simply follow this very simple-to-understand and easy-to-implement technique: buy and pay for things *only* with cash. Don't even use a debit card. Debit cards are convenient, but many cost you money with fees. Did you know the average person *wastes* $200 per year on ATM fees? Crazy! Check your statement! For some reason, *cash* is the new four-letter word. People seem afraid to use it. Cash is clumsy and inconvenient. But, until *cash* becomes obsolete—and I cringe at the day that may happen—*cash* is what runs this country and the world. When you buy and pay with *cash*, you will understand the true value of those dollar bills and the coins in your hand. A debit card cuts out the physiological and psychological response that our body and brain register when we actually touch, feel, count, and smell the money. Later we will discuss how to run your life like a business, and one of the principles in that section is to become fiscally responsible for your financial health. Debt is a big part of it.

In order to reduce and eliminate your debt with this strategy, you must only use cash and hard currency. Use hundred-dollar bills, because when you break a $100 bill, you think harder about what it takes to make that hundred versus a $10 or a $20 bill. Use your biggest bills when you buy things. Try this for a month and watch your debt dwindle. You can reduce your debt *now*.

Paying with cash is not only better for your pocketbook; it also helps the merchant selling you things. When you use a credit or a debit card, the merchant pays a fee to Visa, MasterCard, or American Express, ranging from 1 to 8 percent of the purchase. Before you divulge how you pay for something, ask these questions: What if I pay in cash? Can you work on the price for me? You see, cash not only increases the merchant's bottom line, but also your own bottom line. More times than not, this effective and easy technique will save you money. The other very important benefit for the merchant is the reduced risk of bad debt. It's possible the credit card will be declined, and if it is, the merchant gets charged for that transaction. If a check is written, there is a possibility of insufficient funds or a stop payment on the check. This is also an example of win-win negotiation.

You get the product for less, and the merchant reduces his cost of selling you the goods.

Consider the following scenarios to prove my point.

Heather, a medical professional, was working holidays and pulling overtime as a result of over $55,000 in credit card debt due to medical bills. She tossed and turned countless sleepless nights, juggling the bills in her mind. It took her some time, but she applied the techniques in my book, cut up her credit cards, and climbed out of debt.

By the time she was twenty-eight years old, Shaniqua had amassed close to $30,000 in debt, with about half of it in student loans. Like many young adults, her debt load started when she was eighteen and gleefully got her first clothing store card. She now had sixteen credit cards! She applied the techniques: paying with cash and running her life like a business. She also climbed out of her debt quagmire.

Kristin was buried in credit card debt for years, and her credit score was negatively impacted. She was able to pay only her minimum monthly payment and sometimes used one credit card to pay the other! She applied my principles and in a short period of time reduced almost $100,000 in credit card debt to only $30,000. She increased her credit score and gained a grasp on her financial future. And she did this without credit agencies.

NEGOTIATE YOUR DEBT

While this book is not a "debt book" per se, the totality of the techniques, when combined in a debt situation, will most certainly apply.

You can negotiate your debt, regardless of the type of debt. Let's say you owe one hundred dollars and you want to eliminate it, but you only have sixty dollars. Call the person or company to whom the debt is owed and tell them you can't pay the one hundred dollars, but you can pay sixty right now. Asking to reduce the debt can and does work in many situations, without any negative impact on your credit. You just need to ask. If the offer of paying sixty dollars on a one hundred dollar debt is accepted, you have eliminated forty percent of the debt instantly, and the entire one hundred–dollar debt is now also gone.

THE TOP TWO BIGGEST POTENTIAL SAVERS!

I am a licensed real estate broker in the Commonwealth of Massachusetts: not a mortgage broker, but a real estate broker. I am not an expert by any means, but I know enough about the real estate world to be dangerous. As I mention in television advertisements for *Ask More, Get More*, the two most expensive things people buy in the United States, if not the world, are a car and a house. Next, I discuss the fear of buying these two very important things. And I will also demystify the purchase and sale of these two items by showing you how to be prepared, and I will show you a simple and easy system to apply that will save you thousands if not tens of thousands of dollars. As you will discover later on, this system may actually make you hundreds of thousands, if not millions. Some of the techniques and principles will be discussed in more detail later on in the book.

YOUR HOUSE

I made millions of dollars at a very young age, but I also live a pretty humble life. I live in a small cape house in a modest neighborhood. It is a really nice house to raise my daughter in, and it is located in a neighborhood where she can be a kid and not worry about anything else other than being a kid. Even though my house is modest, I saved thousands of dollars on the purchase price, the renovations, and also the mortgage just by asking the right questions—but more importantly, *asking* for *more*, to *get more*!

When you are buying a house in a typical transaction, you have the *buyer* and the *seller*, and then you also have the *seller's* agent and sometimes the *buyer's* agent. One very simple thing to realize (and this will save you thousands of dollars) is that you do *not* need either one. If you are a *seller* or a *buyer* you can handle the transaction yourself. As I mentioned in my television advertisement, "Real Estate," the concept of real estate is so archaic and complicated that I would not advise jumping into the real estate world as a profession without a solid education. However, if you are buying a house to live in, you can easily do all the research yourself, set appointments to see the property yourself, and negotiate the price yourself. Prior to doing any of this, here are the following steps that will make you and save you thousands of dollars.

Retain a Lawyer in Your Area. People have the misconception that this is expensive, but most real estate lawyers cost no more than a couple thousand dollars, and only get paid at the closing. Among many other things, they will help you draw up a purchase and sales agreement. Too many people make the costly mistake of retaining a lawyer *after* they sign a purchase and sales agreement. This is not advisable. If you get a lawyer after you signed the purchase and sales, or even worse, if you need a lawyer after the purchase and sales, you are in big trouble. Retain a lawyer prior to even looking. An experienced real estate lawyer can walk you through the process prior to actually looking for a home. A brief talk with the lawyer will both save and make you thousands.

Also, since the lawyer is not compensated from the sale price, she is truly in your corner. Real estate agents are ethically obligated to represent their clients, whether the buyer or seller, and disregard their own pecuniary interest. However, I believe this ethical obligation is not uniformly followed, and they are often blinded by their own financial interest. The major difference between the two professions is that a lawyer must graduate law school, pass an ethics exam, *and* pass the bar exam, whereas real estate agents can take an online course, pass a quick test, and *voila!* they are now licensed professionals. When in doubt, go with a lawyer.

Cut Out Third Parties. If you are the *buyer*, cutting out the buyer's agent can save you anywhere from 2 to 4 percent of the purchase price. For a house costing $100,000, that is $2,000-$4,000, which if you paid interest on over thirty years would conservatively cost you $10,000-$20,000. If you are the seller, you can list and show your house on your own. Real estate agents try to make this process confusing or complicated, when it couldn't be easier. I have done it, and know many others who have done it. So, you can list and sell your own home with ease. Homes that are *for sale by owner* are also generally cheaper, and you will not have to deal with brokers.

Research the Area. Of course you would, right? But I have heard horror stories from homebuyers who had no idea that the town they lived in had a horrible school system or that there were plans to have a casino developed the next town over. Buying a home is a very emotional process and should be one that is filled with joy. Buying a home is also a very big deal and usually the biggest purchase of your life. Spend the time to learn everything. Research the school system. Investigate the water supply. Check out the crime rate in surrounding areas. All of this can be done on the Internet.

Research the Homes You Are Considering. If you are looking at a particular home, there are many things you can do to gain an advantage when making the decision to submit an offer. Find the local registry of deeds, which you can use to find almost every document pertaining to that home. Multiple Listing Services, or MLS, is a tool only real estate professionals claim to have access to, but it can also be used by non–real estate professionals. This tool will provide you with a plethora of data on homes. You can see what the current owners paid for their homes; you can find out if they took out a second mortgage, if there are liens, encumbrances, etc. Knowing what the current owners paid is invaluable and can put the whole transaction into perspective. If they bought the home for $300,000 and they are looking for one million, they may be asking for way too much money and would probably be willing to take $500,000. 3 P's + 1 P = Money, peace of mind, and confidence.

State, Federal, or Local Incentives. Most states offer first-time buyer's programs, even on the city level. These incentives can even work for acquiring commercial property. The deals you can get are remarkable. I have a friend who bought an entire commercial building worth over a million dollars from a town—for one dollar! How did he get such a deal? Well, it was in a not-so-glamorous town, but the building was in good condition, and he was bringing jobs to the town. Find out about first-time homebuyer's programs on state, local, and federal levels. Ask what is available in the area. Ask yourself what you are trying to accomplish. Are you looking to raise a family, or just own some property that you can later sell at a profit, allowing you to purchase your dream house?

If it is the latter, consider towns that are not perfect, but where you can purchase property cheap, live comfortably, and build equity. On my website I have a listing of federal agencies that can help you purchase a home.

Explore Different Mortgage Options. The real estate market is a mess due to unethical practices by the big banks and mortgage brokers, who preyed upon vulnerable people who could not afford a home. These people had no idea what it meant to own a home and should not have purchased. This is one of the biggest national scams in the history of the United States, and most of the parties perpetuating this fraud walked away with millions.

There are several types of mortgages that are now available to the American public. When considering these options, think worst-case scenario. What happens when the time comes for mortgage rate increases? What is really going on when I am only paying the interest? What is a balloon payment, and what will happen if I get there? A lot of the mortgages that are available may be a very good tool for a responsible person to get into a house, but you need to ask yourself, "Can I afford the mortgage payment if the adjustable rate goes up? Can I refinance? What happens if I can't make the payments?" The following is an explanation of one of the most common exotic and dangerous mortgages.

Adjustable Rate Mortgage (ARM). ARMs were designed for the very purpose of reducing the monthly mortgage bill for a period of time in order to make home purchases more affordable. There are several different types of ARMs, but the most common is a three-year ARM, where the rate is low for three years, then adjusts to the pre-determined rate. ARMs are great, but you need to ask yourself: "In three years, five years, ten years, will I be able to afford the monthly payment?" With an ARM, usually the principal balance carries over, so even though you are making monthly payments, 99 percent of the payment is going to only interest. As a result you are not really gaining equity unless the real estate market climbs.

On the other hand, what I really like about an ARM is this: You can use an ARM—even if you can make the higher payment in a conventional fixed mortgage—take the difference between the ARM payment and the conventional payment over the three, five, or ten years, and invest it in other vehicles. Right now, I would invest in precious metals and the stock market. People are making a killing presently in both. One basic, simple, and easy way to get in the stock market is to max your 401k contribution (if you have one), start a Roth IRA, or buy some mutual funds. Essentially, the ARM gives you the option of putting money into other vehicles for the first three years of the mortgage. In the long run, this will actually make you more money.

QUICK TIPS

> If you are dealing with a buyer's or seller's agent, ask the agent to reduce the commission rate.

> Negotiate the price, no matter what. My rule of thumb is offer 30 percent less than what they are asking. It is not offensive and will most likely elicit a response.

> Look for foreclosures, bank-owned properties, and short sales. You can get amazing deals. On my website, I have a list of great websites that can help you find these in your area.

> If you go with a conventional mortgage, see what a fifteen-year fixed mortgage monthly payment looks like, as it will save you tens of thousands in interest.

> Pay something—anything—each month toward the principal, and make sure you designate the additional payment as a "principal payment," or it may just be applied to interest.

> Look for local incentives to buy; ask about first-time homebuyer incentives and veterans' benefits.

> Be prepared to walk away if the deal isn't right.

YOUR AUTOMOBILE

Later on in the book I further discuss my illustrious career as a car salesman, where I learned many things. My advice comes from a few years of day-to-day experience. I know that buying a car is also a very emotional purchase. We spend a significant part of our lives in a car, and we as human beings have an affinity for the automobile. One of the first things—and I believe the most important thing—to do when purchasing a car is to take the emotion out of the purchase. You can take the emotion out of the purchasing decision by asking questions *before* you walk into a dealership.

Over the past ten years the car purchasing experience has changed significantly. Since the beginnings of the Internet, consumers have become educated and savvy. Over the Internet, you can compare cars, do virtual tours, get the invoice, hire companies to buy the car for you, and even buy the car without ever walking into the dealership. Even though consumers are now armed with the Internet tools, purchasing a car can still be complicated. The more questions you ask, the more you will save.

Buying a new car versus buying a used car are two completely different types of transactions, and when you have a trade, the transaction becomes more complicated. And leasing involves a different type of transaction. I discuss each scenario in greater length on my website, but the following list is designed to get you to *ask more* questions before you walk into the dealership in order to *get more*. Later on there are techniques that you will learn that should be applied as well.

QUICK TIPS

› Cut out all emotion.

› Know exactly why you want the car.

› Get the invoice and find out about all incentives, including incentives the manufacturer is giving to the dealerships.

› Check consumer reports for safety and reliability.

› Ask yourself how much can you afford, and never go over it.

› Ask yourself how you will feel in the vehicle three years later. A lot of people get out of their car three years later and they are upside down, meaning the amount owed is greater than what the car is actually worth.

› Get quotes from online dealerships in writing. Still very difficult to do, but understand that these quotes are usually not the bottom-line price.

› Shop price; go to several dealerships with the firm decision that you are not buying, no matter what the deal. Take out the emotion!

› When you finally settle on a car, test drive the car, and if the car is used, take the car to your mechanic. If you do nothing else, take the car to your mechanic. This will save you thousands. Ask the mechanic this question: "If you were me, would you buy this car?"

› Research the dealership; go to the Better Business Bureau and see if they have a good rating. If not, don't bother walking through the doors.

› When you are ready to make the purchasing decision, do it on the last day of the month. Yes, you really will get a better deal then. In fact, go in later in the day on the last day of the month.

› When you enter the dealership, ask to speak with the manager. They will then give you a salesperson who is usually no-nonsense.

› Negotiate price, not payment (leasing is different). Since you have done your homework, you will know what the payment will be, based upon the price.

> Even though you know the invoice and all of the incentives, offer 20 percent less than the invoice.

> Never tell the salesperson that you have done your homework. Claiming ignorance can work to your advantage.

> Negotiate the trade after you negotiate the price of your car. Dealerships will inflate what you think you are getting on your trade due to the markup on the car you are buying.

These tips may all seem like common sense, but in my experience, when people walk into the dealership, emotion takes over and rational thought goes out the window. As a result, the skills that you are learning in *Ask More, Get More* are forgotten. Don't let emotion take over, and when you finish the book, the strategies and techniques that you will have learned, coupled with the tips in this section, will get you the best deal you have ever gotten on a car, and you will feel good about it.

SAVINGS UNLIMITED!

My other book, *Reduce Debt Now* (available on my website), contains the exact way to reduce your debt, and this chapter expounds on some of those principles while highlighting a few new ones. However, it is the totality of the concepts, techniques, and principles in *Reduce Debt Now* that will reduce and even eliminate your debt. From going on vacation for free, to understanding how and when to ask the right questions, you will reduce your debt and possibly eliminate it. If your goal is to lower debt, do not just rely on this chapter—incorporate the entire book into your debt reduction or elimination plan.

TAXES

I am by no means a tax expert, and I suggest you consult with an accountant before you make any decisions, but you need to prepare for taxes as if they were due now. Tax preparation should not be something that you prepare when it's time to file. The tax code changes every year, but a few simple things can be done to save you and make you a lot of money. I also believe that even though the tax code is complicated and often changing, programs like Turbo Tax are a great tool and can save you the fee that a tax service agency would charge you.

PAY TO SAVE!

This advice may seem crazy, but you can make energy-efficient improvements to your home and qualify for a credit of up to 30 percent of the cost, with a maximum credit of $1,500. Insulation, energy-efficient windows, and heating and air-conditioning systems all qualify. These credits seem to change from year to year, so check with your tax adviser, but you can buy things for your home that save you money, and essentially get things like windows for *free*!

CHARITABLE DONATIONS

If you contribute to your church, your local colleges, the local dog pound, the United Way, and/or various organizations that help with disaster relief, be sure to make these donations throughout the year, and don't wait. Later on we discuss giving back. Regardless of your financial situation, it is always great to give back. Not only are there tax benefits, but what goes around does come around, and it also is just the right thing to do. Don't be careless with your charitable gifts; get receipts so that you will have them when it's time to file. Charitable organizations understand that your contributions are tax deductible, so *always* ask for a receipt and keep a record of it.

TIP: If you don't have the cash . . .

Find out whether the organization can process a donation via credit card. As long as the donation is made by December 31, it's a valid deduction that year, even if you don't pay your credit card bill until next year. However, I would only recommend this if your credit card bills are under control.

MORTGAGE INTEREST

If you are fortunate enough to own a home and have money available to do so, make your January 1 mortgage payment by December 31 of the previous year. The downside is that you won't be able to deduct the payment from your following year's return, but you can keep rolling it each year during the life of your mortgage.

REAL ESTATE TAXES

If you pay your own real estate taxes, make any payments due in the beginning of the new year by December 31 of the current year.

My taxes are taken out monthly with each mortgage payment. I am, unfortunately, not able to take advantage of this technique.

CAPITAL GAINS AND LOSSES

As I write this book, 2011 has been a wild ride for investments and will most certainly end leaving us with more questions than answers. Over time, the market will show a return, so investing $25 is still like making $7,225. This can seem a little complicated, but remember this: if you have capital gains, remember that any net capital losses over the $3,000 allowed on this year's tax return should be carried forward to offset those following years' gains. If you still have net losses, up to $3,000 may be used to offset ordinary income for the current year.

Also, remember that when you have a capital gain from an investment, you pay substantially less taxes. Just ask Warren Buffet, who has been pretty vocal about his tax bracket. Warren Buffet, one of the richest men in the world, pays a lower tax rate than his secretary, because his income is derived from investments. This is a big secret of the rich. Warren Buffet, who is now a billionaire, pays roughly 17 percent in taxes, while his secretary pays close to 36 percent. Buffet has been making noise about this for a few years, but you didn't hear him making this noise when he was on his way up. This was and, quite frankly, still is a well-guarded secret of the rich. Despite what the media coverage is or may be in the future, people don't understand how to invest and make money. But, you now know it is possible and can be done. Want to pay less in taxes?

INVEST!

The pieces of advice mentioned above are just a few basic things to consider when filing or preparing taxes. In the spirit of *Ask More, Get More*, I urge you to spend a little time now preparing for the future and educating yourself, so that you can *ask* the right questions to maximize your tax benefit. The rich use the tax code to their advantage, and that's only because they *ask more*. You should too! There are many other things that can be done, and the tax code is constantly changing, so pay attention. You can also find more tips at www.AskMore-GetMore.com.

IF YOU OWE TAXES OR HAVE A TAX LIEN ON YOUR PROPERTY

The Internal Revenue Service (IRS) is a scary government agency. They are probably the most powerful agency within the executive branch of the United States government. You hear all sorts of horror stories about people losing their homes and their businesses. Then there are those frightening commercials: "Do you owe the IRS money? Are they showing up at your home or business? If so, then don't go at it alone; we will 'settle' your tax liability." If you listen closely, they just say that they are going to "settle" your tax problem. The truth is that *you* can settle your own tax problem.

The IRS doesn't advertise the fact that you can reduce your tax obligation and even avoid penalties, although there is information on their website. One thing that the IRS does offer is called an Offer in Compromise (OIC) in which you pay a nominal fee and submit an offer to settle for less money than is owed. The IRS can legally reduce your tax obligation for one of the following reasons:

> Doubt as to liability: if you can raise doubt as to the exact amount owed.

> Doubt as to collectability: There is doubt that you could *ever* pay the full amount.

> Promoting effective tax administration: I like this one; it basically acknowledges that you do in fact owe money but you have a hardship or other special circumstances, which would prevent you from paying the full amount.

There are three types of OICs:

> Lump Sum Cash: You agree on an amount and you pay the lump sum within five or fewer installments from the notice of acceptance.

> Short Term Periodic Payment: This is basically a payment plan at an agreed upon amount for two years.

> Deferred Periodic Payment: Can be paid out longer than twenty-four months, but must be paid within ten years.

The OIC is not always accepted, but can be appealed. You can learn more about the OIC on my website www.AskMore-GetMore.com or at www.irs.gov.

DON'T LET IT BECOME A MENTAL MONSTER

I have a relative who has his own small business. And although he is a great carpenter, he is admittedly not a good bookkeeper. For ten years, he neglected to file tax returns. He did this because he was living hand-to-mouth, barely scraping by, and thought he would end up owing money to the IRS should he actually file his taxes. So he just never filed and just kept running the business. This carried on until the day when the big, bad IRS showed up in a *big* way. They put a lien on his house, and guess what? IRS agents started showing up at that house and threatening to take it. He was petrified. We talked about this dilemma, and there were many mistakes that he made along the way.

Number one, he was acting as a sole proprietor. Thus, he was putting all of his personal assets at risk because he did not want to "waste time" by forming a corporation or a limited liability company.

Number two, he didn't have a bookkeeper who logged his income and expenses.

Number three—and this was the reason for a lot of his fear—he never filed taxes.

So, he finally got over the fear, went to a tax accountant, and filed his taxes. To his pleasant surprise, not only did he not owe money, but he was due money! He was shocked! For almost ten years, he was living in constant fear of losing his home—needlessly.

I have another relative who barely makes enough money to feed his family. This relative has not only decided not to file taxes for years, he also claimed too many dependents and did, in fact, owe money. He was trying to stretch the dollar he was earning by not filing. Well, those penalties and the interest do not go away; in fact, they get worse. This family member has his already meager wages attached by the IRS, plus he has to pay child support. Each week he barely has enough money to put gas in his car to get to work!

File your taxes and deal with the situation now, rather than waiting. Most of the horror stories you hear involving people losing their homes or assets are a result of being ill-prepared and just waiting until it is too late. Quickly pull the Band-Aid off! It may hurt or sting, but in the long term your wounds will heal.

The IRS will work with you no matter what the situation. Several years ago, I got hit with an unexpected tax bill, and I did not have nearly enough money to pay it. Rather than just tossing the notice in the garbage and acting like it didn't exist, I called the IRS. I worked out a plan with them and turned what was a fairly large tax bill into a zero-dollar tax burden rather quickly.

If you get a notice or if the IRS shows up at your place of work or home, you need to remain calm and treat the other person with respect. They are just doing their job and are not "out to get you." When you discuss your tax challenge with them, be honest when describing your situation, and they will work with you. Ask to have the penalties and interests waived, and inquire about working out a payment plan. Even if you enter into a payment plan and you can't make that payment, communicate with them. Nobody likes to pay taxes, but taxes are a part of your life, so you have to deal with them. Be nice, be honest, treat the other person with respect, and you will find that your tax challenge will soon be a thing of the past.

ASK YOURSELF: ARE YOU USING AND PAYING TOO MUCH FOR YOUR WATER?

Water bills vary by state, county, and town but range from $15–60 a month per household. When I was conducting research for this book, I told one of my research interns a technique I've used since I was a kid and he looked at me like I was crazy. After the research was over, he got the picture. In the United States, we flush close to five *billion* gallons of water every day! The toilet uses the most water in the household, accounting for a little more than 26 percent of the daily water usage.

Household Size	Gallons	HCF (hundreds of cubic feet)
1 person	748 to 2,244	1 to 3
2 person	2,992 to 5,236	4 to 7
3 person	5,984 to 7,480	8 to 10
4 person	8,228 to 9,724	11 to 13
5 person	10,472 to 11,968	14 to 16
6 person	12,716 to 14,212	17 to 19

The average toilet uses 1.6 gallons of water per flush. During the course of a day, that adds up to a fair amount of water. One way to reduce your toilet's consumption is to reduce the amount of water it uses per flush. When placed in the tank, an ordinary brick will displace roughly a quart of the water it takes to fill up the tank. Over the course of a day, those quarts can add up to several gallons of water per day, per week, per month, and eventually per year. You could also double up and use two bricks. Most towns now require homeowners to install new modern, more efficient toilets. You can often get a rebate for installing a toilet that uses less water. If you don't want to spend $300–500 for a new toilet, use the brick trick to save water and money.

Showers account for about 17 percent of water usage, with the washer accounting for about 22 percent. For many of us, the shower is the only time we relax. We sit under the scalding hot water until the heat runs out. Ask yourself: How much could I save and ultimately make if I spent a little less time in the shower? Would you be able to relax more if your water bill was cut in half? One thing I do at my house that reduces my water bills is to always shower at the gym. I figure I pay a monthly bill anyway, why use my water when I can use theirs?

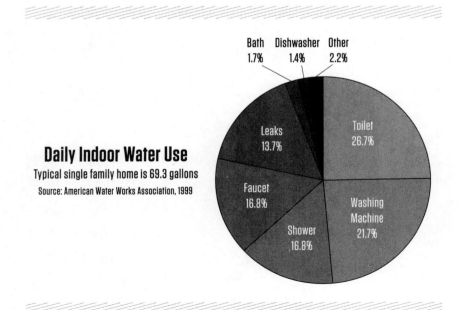

Daily Indoor Water Use
Typical single family home is 69.3 gallons
Source: American Water Works Association, 1999

Bath 1.7% Dishwasher 1.4% Other 2.2%

Leaks 13.7%

Toilet 26.7%

Faucet 16.8%

Washing Machine 21.7%

Shower 16.8%

SAVE MORE BY ASKING YOURSELF AND YOUR UTILITY A FEW QUESTIONS

As I mentioned in a television advertisement for *Ask More, Get More,* in the late 1970s several states began to deregulate both electricity and natural gas. Honestly, I had no idea this existed until a few years ago, when I was researching a company that was marketing its services for reduced electricity rates. Electricity and gas are things that you *pay* for, and you can use the phrases, techniques, and strategies in this book to reduce your rates significantly. The utility companies have done a great job for close to forty years of keeping this deregulation a secret, and they are not going to be happy when they read this book. The following list identifies which states have deregulated their electricity and gas industries, and which states still regulate both.

You can go to www.AskMore-GetMore.com for a list of companies in your state that provide you with options.

	Electricity	Gas
Alabama	No	No
Alaska	No	No
Arizona	Yes	No
Arkansas	Yes	No
California	Yes	PC—Partial Choice
Connecticut	Yes	No
Colorado	No	No
Delaware	Yes	PC—Partial Choice

	Electricity	Gas
Florida	No	Yes
Georgia	No	Yes
Hawaii	No	No
Idaho	No	No
Illinois	Yes	Yes
Indiana	No	Yes
Iowa	No	Yes
Kansas	No	No
Kentucky	No	No
Louisiana	No	No
Maine	Yes	No
Maryland	Yes	Yes
Massachusetts	Yes	Yes
Michigan	Yes	Yes
Minnesota	No	No
Mississippi	No	No
Missouri	No	PC—Partial Choice
Montana	Yes	Yes
Nebraska	No	No
Nevada	Yes	Yes
New Hampshire	Yes	No
New Jersey	Yes	Yes
New Mexico	Yes	Yes
New York	Yes	Yes
North Carolina	No	No

	Electricity	Gas
North Dakota	No	No
Ohio	Yes	Yes
Oklahoma	Yes	No
Oregon	Yes	No
Pennsylvania	Yes	Yes
Rhode Island	Yes	Yes
South Carolina	No	No
South Dakota	No	No
Tennessee	No	No
Texas	Yes	PC—Partial Choice
Utah	No	No
Vermont	No	No
Virginia	Yes	Yes
Washington	No	No
Washington, DC	Yes	Yes
West Virginia	No	Yes
Wisconsin	No	No
Wyoming	No	PC—Partial Choice

The reason the utility companies were deregulated was because they were a monopoly, and a monopoly is never good for the consumer. Don't be afraid of changing your electricity supplier, as the electricity you receive is the same from supplier to supplier. Your electricity and natural gas will continue to be delivered safely and reliably by the local utility company—a company still regulated by the Public Utility Commission. With deregulation, you have the option to pay less—sometimes up to 50 percent less! The average household spends $105 per month on electricity. If you could save $50 a month—$600 a year—by making a quick and easy change, this book would pay for itself twenty times over! Saving money is making money! And this is just electricity!

What if you are a renter and your electric or gas is included? Ask your landlord to look at the energy providers, and provide them with options to reduce cost. Then ask the landlord to reduce your monthly rent proportional to the energy savings.

Now, we are just talking about switching to a different provider. If you call your supplier and use the skills, phrases, and techniques in the book, you may not need to switch. In addition to using the easily applied skills and techniques in the book with your supplier, the following are some tips that can reduce your total electric bill, regardless of the supplier. On my website, AskMore-GetMore.com, I include additional tips and discuss some cool devices to help reduce costs and make you money!

MORE ENERGY SAVING—MONEY SAVING—TIPS!

The term "electricity vampire" references household items that constantly drain energy and ultimately cost you money even if they are off. Things like your TV, your phone charger, a blow-dryer, a computer, a lamp, toaster, microwave, or a stereo can all suck electricity and cost you money. The first thing you need to do is get into the habit of unplugging them every day or night. Another great thing to do is purchase a power-bar or a mat with timer settings on them—also known as a power mat. With a power mat you can charge multiple things at once. With a power bar, you can plug multiple items in, but the timer shuts them off and essentially disconnects them from the wall. Ever notice that your DVD player or TV may have an LED light on showing that it is "off"? That light doesn't magically appear; it takes electricity and costs you money. The devices that are shut off but still plugged in are responsible for anywhere from 5–10 percent of the average household electric bill!

TIP: Thinking of buying a computer? Pack up those old desktops in favor of the more lightweight and energy-efficient laptops. They consume less than one-third of the energy with almost all of the benefits of a desktop, and with the advent of wireless technology, you can use them all over your house.

You have probably seen those lightbulbs that look like a small, curled-up snake. Well, these squirrelly little fluorescent lightbulbs use 78 percent less electricity than the round ones you have been buying since the beginning of time. They give you the same amount of light output, cost you less, and are safer. They don't produce as much heat, and when broken, they do not shatter all over the place like the ones you bought from Thomas Edison.

If you still have an old tube-TV? Well, this is a great reason to get the flat screen you have been yearning for. LCD TVs use significantly less energy, and many of them are already Energy Star–rated. Plus, the flat-screen TVs are rapidly dropping in price. Opt for an LCD over a plasma TV, as plasma TVs use more energy and are not as reliable.

When I started to write *Ask More, Get More*, I looked at my own personal electricity situation. For some reason, my family used more electricity than anyone in my neighborhood. I thought I was doing all the right things, and I couldn't figure out why our bill was barely moving south. One huge draw on our electric bill was an old refrigerator in our garage that we use as a spare and for storing excess food. We actually got the fridge for free! Well, that fridge has probably cost me three times what it was worth! I switched to an Energy Star freezer and watched my bill drop noticeably! If you are considering a refrigerator purchase, make sure it is Energy Star–rated. The same goes for your washer and dryer. When I bought my house, we negotiated the washer and dryer as part of the purchase. Several years ago, that was a good deal, but long-term if I had kept that dryer, my "free" dryer would have actually cost me.

ONE MAN'S TRASH IS ANOTHER MAN'S WAY OF ASKING FOR MORE

After I properly disassembled the refrigerator, I assumed the garbage men would take it. I didn't have time to find out. The morning of trash day, a short, middle-aged Hispanic man knocked on my door and asked for my help. When I looked past my driveway, he had an old, small-cab Chevy pickup full of scrap metal parked next to my garbage. The reason why he knocked was that my old refrigerator was worth something to him.

As I approached the man's pickup, which was overflowing with junk and the refrigerator at the end of the bed of his truck, I realized the refrigerator would not fit, but he was determined to get it on his truck. We rearranged the items in his vehicle and then put the refrigerator on top of his truck. As we were moving the refrigerator around all the sharp pieces of metal and old lawn mowers, I noticed that this man was missing two fingers on his left hand, and I was impressed with his strength for a man who barely stood five feet.

After the refrigerator was successfully loaded onto the truck, I told him that it wasn't safe, and he couldn't drive away without it being secure. I told him to hold on, and I got a rope to help secure the refrigerator on top of his small, overflowing Chevy pickup. Once we finally got the refrigerator secure, I asked him his name, and he said José. I shook his hand and was proud to know him for that brief moment. He went on to tell me that he would get about $30 for the refrigerator, and that he gets about $150 a day in scrap metal, driving from town to town on different trash days.

José didn't care what I thought or what other people thought of him. José has a family to feed and basic living expenses to pay. He is disabled and speaks little English, but he used inner strength and creative thinking to find a way to put food on his table and money in his pocket. José is a fine example of human ingenuity, drive, and desire. I didn't spend a lot of time with José, but anyone can apply the skills that we all have from within to not only survive, but to prosper.

And you can do the same if you apply the strategies and techniques in this book and absorb its principles. You can save money on the basic things in your life like water, electricity, food, gas, and anything else you pay for or purchase. You can also apply the strategies to every aspect of your life so that you can have a better life, just as José was determined to have. On my website, I have many saving techniques that are invaluable, but not appropriate for the book. There are literally hundreds of things you can do to reduce your water and electric bills, but ultimately it goes back to the basics you will learn in the book. When you understand that saving fifty dollars a month is like making almost $15,000, you will begin to realize that, regardless of your current financial situation, you can and should make and save money. These techniques work both in the short-term and long-term. Nike said it best: *Just do it!* Think just a little differently, and you will change your financial future.

PART III

ASK MORE FROM LIFE

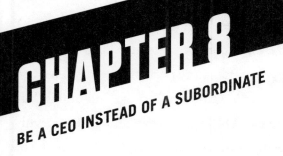

CHAPTER 8
BE A CEO INSTEAD OF A SUBORDINATE

IS THAT HOW YOU WANT TO BE REMEMBERED?

As I have stated throughout the book, when I was a kid I struggled with doing the right thing. I used to get into fights a lot. I generally would not start the altercations, but I used to fight almost daily. Most of the time it was another teenager trying to prove how tough he was; I was and am a big guy, so others were constantly challenging me. One day I was in the next town over from where I grew up with some of my friends, and we met a group of other teenagers. We did not know them, but after introductions they knew me. They knew me because of my reputation as a tough street kid. When I got home I proudly told my mother that I was known to these kids from another town. She asked me how they knew me. I told her it was because they heard of how tough I was. My mom then looked at me and said, "Is that how you want to be remembered?" I was fourteen or fifteen at the time, and that question hit me hard. Is that how I want to be remembered—as just a tough guy?

I then started asking myself questions almost immediately. How far will this take me in life? *Where* will this take me in life? Where will I end up? As I tried to answer the questions I was asking myself, I knew that being a tough guy was not going to lead to good things. I did get into some scuffles after that fateful day, but they were literally self-defense. As I began to get more involved with sports and academics, the fighting dissipated, and to this day I ask myself a modified version of my mother's question: How do I want to be remembered?

I CAN BUY AN ICE CREAM

This past summer I was at a local beach with my daughter, and we were buying some ice cream. We were looking over the different flavors and we each picked what we wanted. We each got cookies and cream with sprinkles, both smalls; she got hers on a sugar cone and I got mine in a cup. After we paid, we were sitting down at a bench right next to the service window. As we were blissfully enjoying our ice cream, an old woman slowly walked up to the window. She appeared to be reviewing the flavors, and then I heard her ask how much the small was. After hearing the price she looked down into her hand and then sadly walked away. This woman was probably in her eighties, and I could tell from her body language that she was upset because she couldn't afford the ice cream.

It hit me so hard that this woman either could not afford an ice cream or made the decision not to buy the ice cream because it didn't fit into her budget. I was saddened by witnessing this, but I was also so appreciative that I can buy an ice cream for my daughter and me whenever we want. I can pretty much buy anything we want or need without looking at the price (but I always do) or doing the math in my head to see if we can afford it.

The simple things in life, the things that I, too, couldn't afford when I was a kid, I can now enjoy. Funny thing is, when I was a kid and could not afford an ice cream, my friends and I would collect cans, cash them in, and go to the local Dairy Queen. They had a cool program called the "Mistake." Mistakes were ice creams, ice cream floats, frappes, or other ice cream concoctions that for some reason or another were mistakenly made and then put in the freezer. For *ten cents* you could go to the ice cream window and ask for a Mistake without knowing what you would get. Sometimes you would get a banana split or a small vanilla with rainbow sprinkles. But we didn't care! *Ten cents* for ice cream bliss.

But I digress . . . the important point is that it wasn't too long ago where I would get anxiety when going through a cashier stand and not knowing whether or not my credit card would be declined. In fact, many times I would make a joke before they ran it and say things like, "I hope I didn't forget to pay the bill," to alleviate any potential embarrassment. Today when my credit card is declined, I still get the uneasy feeling of what it felt like to not be able to buy a real ice cream. But now I know it is usually my credit card company protecting the card, or it's some mistake.

But the fear of not being able to pay is still with me and also drives me to continue to make sure that I will always be able to buy my little girl an ice cream. Ask yourself: Wouldn't it feel great to not worry about what things cost? Or worry about how you will pay for things? You can do it by following the many techniques in my book and simply by *asking* more out of life.

HOW TO RUN YOUR LIFE LIKE A BUSINESS: BE THE CEO OF YOU ENTERPRISES, INC.

Robert Kiyosaki, in *Rich Dad, Poor Dad*, says that people need to "mind their own business." Too many people work for a company or for a person, and they don't think of their life as a business. In *Rich Dad, Poor Dad* he tells a story about Ray Kroc and what his "business" was. Ray Kroc's business was building real estate, while his profession was salesman of McDonald's franchises. You need to understand that your profession is what you are doing right now (or want to do), but your business is *you*.

Do you ever wonder what "rich people" do to get there? Joan Rivers had a show that was on TV for a little bit that was a bit like Robin Leach's show, *Lifestyles of the Rich and Famous*. Her show was called *How'd You Get So Rich?* I thought it was a brilliant concept; she would appear at the front door of large estates and ask the person who answered, "How'd you get so rich?" I didn't watch every episode, but in all the ones I watched, the people became rich by owning their own businesses and running their personal lives like a business.

Before I started Blue Vase Marketing, LLC (www.bluevasellc.com) a few years ago, I studied the habits of other rich and successful people and how they maintained their wealth and success. I also studied people who made it and then lost it. The difference between the two is that the people who kept their wealth set up their personal life like a business.

When I was in law school I cringed at taking classes like Wills and Trusts, and Trusts and Estates. In fact, I didn't even know what a trust was. You always hear of trust fund babies; have you ever met a poor trust fund baby? No, you haven't. That is because these trust fund babies were the beneficiary of family members, usually parents or grandparents, who set up their personal life like a business, enabling them to take care of the beneficiary. I have been studying the personal lives of many rich and successful people, and when I was able to peek behind the curtains, I was amazed at the level of sophistication and surprised how easy it was to set up and organize your personal life in a way that seemed complex, but in reality was very easy.

Another very interesting thing I have noticed is that middle-class or poor people don't think they need things like trusts, wills, life insurance, or some other things that "rich people" have. I, too, once thought a trust or a will was just too difficult to understand or manage. Setting up a trust, having a will, or having life insurance are simple tools, and in most instances very inexpensive. They will protect you and your family, save your family's money, and prepare your family for the future. There are too many legal cases that create heartache, litigation, and many times tear families apart because the deceased did not set up his or her life like a business.

A good friend of mine recently lost his dad, who passed away without a will. His father wasn't a wealthy man, but he had some land in Louisiana. This land was swampland; but lo and behold, after some geological surveys were conducted, it just so happens this land sits on a very large natural gas reserve and potential oil. The land is potentially worth millions, and a major energy company wants to lease the land. The problem is, due to the fact that my friend's dad "didn't think he needed a will," this land could be tied up in land and probate court for years, causing not only heartache, but also costing him a lot of money in legal fees. It may seem coldhearted, but the fact is, if my friend's dad had run his life like a business, he would have had things like a will, a trust, and life insurance.

If you think that you don't need things like wills, trusts, and life insurance, then you need to change the way you think. You are your own natural gas and oil reserve, and you need to protect *you*. If you don't have assets and money right now, you will soon. Your life is your personal business, and just like eating healthy and exercising in order to live longer, you need to properly set up your personal life to ensure the financial health of YOU Enterprises, Inc. and to prepare yourself for future success.

YOU ARE THE CEO OF YOU ENTERPRISES, INC.

A chief executive officer (CEO) has to make tough decisions; if not, the company could collapse. Your own life could face similar problems if, as the CEO of YOU Enterprises, Inc., you don't make the tough decisions. As you have already read, you must take responsibility for your own life. You can think of this as a kind of sole proprietorship. That means you have to be honest with yourself first. If you can't be honest with yourself and look at things objectively, then your success in almost any venture will be hampered and difficult to obtain.

I once heard a psychologist explain why the American economy and the world economy essentially collapsed. He said, in more eloquent and clinical terms, that the national debt of the United States is so huge and out of control that as human beings, politicians' natural defense mechanisms kick in and don't allow for them to actually deal with the situation (some people would disagree that politicians are human). He went on to say that if the human brain were to attempt to handle this situation, the flight-defense part of our brain would be so strained that we as human beings would essentially have a mental breakdown. So rather than dealing with the situation, we just keep pushing it away. We procrastinate. Procrastination is another disease that leads to failure, and if not put in check can turn into a *mental monster*!

PREPARE LIKE NEXT WEEK IS CHRISTMAS

I discovered something that is fairly obvious, but that we rarely think about. When I was analyzing my company's year-end sales, I noticed that the week before Christmas our sales were down significantly. I decided to look back at previous years and noticed the same thing. I asked all of my executive team why this was, and even talked to individual sales professionals. They all had the same answer: people were Christmas shopping and saving in order to make sure they could buy gifts for friends and family members.

Then, while I was reviewing bonuses for my employees, I observed that my employees were not only waiting for their bonuses, but depending on them so they could pay for Christmas gifts. It then hit me like a Mack truck: What if we as a society prepared every week as if the following week were Christmas? The reason why my sales were down—and probably always will be—a week or so before Christmas is because people are "saving" or "preparing" for the holiday. Many times, people are not prepared, and as a result they use that fabulous plastic thing in our wallets that allows us to forget what is really happening to our financial future—the credit card. A friend of mine who owns a company gave out bonuses even though he couldn't financially justify it. I asked him why. He answered that we as a society believe it is important to try to give gifts, even to our own personal financial detriment. And that is what happens when you don't prepare and end up using your credit card for gifts. You are actually paying more for the gift by using a credit card. Any creditable financial adviser will tell you to never pay for a vacation or gifts on a credit card, with two small caveats: if you get points and if you can pay it off.

Moving forward, prepare each week like the following week is Christmas, and you will find that you will cut out unnecessary items from your personal budget. Zig Ziglar said in *See You at the Top* that you should work every day like you are going on vacation the next day, and you will get a lot more accomplished. Work each week like the following week is Christmas, and you will find that you save more, have more flexibility, and are more prepared.

TIP: Christmas Clubs.

If your company offers one, take advantage of it. It forces you to prepare for a time that is already stressful.

BE HONEST WITH YOUR PERSONAL BUSINESS

One of my first "real" businesses was created from an idea I had in college. Like many college students, I did my fair share of drinking, and in my senior year we were doing shots and chasing the shots with freeze pops. It came to me one night—the great idea of combining alcohol with the freeze pops. After I graduated college, one of the first things I did when I got home was buy a chemistry kit, sort of the kind you got when you were a kid. I began to experiment with different formulations. I was trying to find the perfect ratio so that the freeze pop would freeze.

Now, I knew *nothing* about chemistry or the liquor business, but I had a great, million-dollar idea, and I was not going to let it slip by. I was not going to be that guy who said, "If I had only tried that idea, I wonder what would have happened?" I was going to take a risk.

After a few weeks I found the proper ratio of juice to alcohol. They froze solid, were 8.2 percent alcohol, and tasted great! I invented a freeze pop called Zeus Juice that was infused with alcohol and froze solid. Genius!

As I began to explore what it took to run a business and began to study things like capital, sales projections, and marketing, I met someone who gave me some pretty sound advice. Unfortunately, I didn't listen. This person told me that whatever you think you need for capital, multiply it by three; and boy, were they right.

More importantly, this individual said that when you are evaluating a business venture, ask yourself two very important questions: 1) Has anyone else thought of the idea? 2) If they had thought of the idea, are they still doing it? To my surprise, I learned I wasn't the first one who thought of this. In fact, I found several companies that had tried making frozen alcoholic popsicles. One company was even having success overseas with the idea, but not in the United States. I decided to not ask any more questions. I didn't apply the 3 P's + 1 P technique, and I pushed forward. That was a big mistake, and I paid dearly. Many other companies had tried my idea, and all failed for one reason or another. Some truly failed. Some tried and gave up. And the one company overseas was having major legal challenges trying to get their product into the United States. I saw this as my opportunity to beat them to the market, and I did! I spent close to $100,000 getting a freeze pop infused with alcohol approved by the Bureau of Alcohol, Tobacco, Firearms and Explosives and licensed in many of the states. Ultimately, I ran out of capital because I didn't listen to my friend—who was and is a very successful businessman. And I did not ask enough questions. I wish the story ended there.

I was forced to file for bankruptcy and to shut the business down. It was a horrible feeling, and I felt defeated. Filing for bankruptcy has a stigma and hurts your credit for ten years, but I was forced to make the tough decision with my personal life—also known as ME Enterprises, Inc. Filing bankruptcy is one technique with which you can eliminate your debt. By filing bankruptcy I eliminated over $200,000 in debt. Bankruptcy is a great option for people who took a chance like I did; it gives you a second chance. Consider bankruptcy when necessary to give yourself a fresh start. But do not abuse bankruptcy; many people file for bankruptcy simply because they are living a lifestyle that they should not have.

But the important thing is that even though that one endeavor didn't work, the business that is "me" did! A few years later, I found some investors, asked myself all the right questions, applied 3 P's + 1 P, analyzed why other others were not successful, and formed a new company. As I type today, we are approved in thirteen states, and we have the infrastructure set up to really take Zeus Juice to market.

GET REAL PERSONAL

Earlier in the book, I discussed insanity as defined by Albert Einstein, and I think so many of us actually suffer with insanity as it relates to our personal finances. You have to ask yourself tough questions that you may not want to hear the answer to. When you are able to do that, you will be in a much better position to evaluate your business and make the right decisions.

Ask yourself questions like:

› Am I spending more than I make? For most, the answer is yes.
› Am I living beyond my means?
› Does my partner (spouse) know our real financial situation?
› Am I doing everything I can to reduce my costs?

Once you find the answers to the questions, you have to do something different to make the necessary changes. Waiting will make it worse. The more you put it off, the more it becomes a *mental monster*. Do not let your personal business become a mental monster; it doesn't have to be. The following are some additional tough questions, listed in no particular order. Most people don't like to ask themselves these questions, but if you do and answer them honestly, you can begin to become financially free.

› Do I have a five-year plan? A ten-year plan? Fifteen, twenty, etc.?
› If I were to stop bringing in income today, how long could I sustain my current lifestyle?
› Do I have enough money set aside for emergencies?
› Am I saving enough money?
› Do I spend money on things I shouldn't, like cigarettes, alcohol, or drugs?
› Am I saving for my child's education?
› Do I have a daily, weekly, and monthly budget?

> › What is my financial net worth? If I paid all my debts, what would be left over?

I'm sure you can come up with more questions, and you should. Once you can face and answer the tough questions, the ones you *don't* want to hear the answers to, you can then address the questions and change course, allowing you to cure your personal financial insanity. *Ask more* questions and *get more* out of your personal business. Don't let your personal financial situation turn into a mental monster that could become impossible to defeat; ask questions *now*!

Some say that it is depressing to know their true financial picture. They don't want to face the fact that they are working day after day, not getting anywhere, going deeper into debt, and that their future does not look bright. But if you don't learn about your financial troubles now, when you finally decide to make the decision to ask yourself the tough questions it will be that much more difficult to reverse the damage that was being caused because of your lack of personal accountability and refusal to ask tough questions. Remember, you are the CEO of YOU Enterprises, Inc. and *you* need to be able to make the tough decisions and ask the tough questions in order for your business—your life—to thrive.

YOUR CASH FLOW

As I mentioned earlier, my father is a machinist, the classic, hardworking, lower-middle-class guy, always trying to stretch his paycheck a little bit further, but just barely getting by. One thing I learned from him when I was a kid was that every weekend he used to handwrite—with a pencil so he could adjust—his bills and his cash flow. My parents are divorced, and I would see my dad on the weekends. He would essentially create a cash flow projection for his personal life. Almost always it was in the red.

But his income is not the point. He did not hide behind the fact that his bills were growing faster than his income; he wrote down in a pretty organized manner what was owed and what he had. This is the first step to running your personal life like a business.

BUT DON'T BE OVERCAUTIOUS—GO FOR IT!

"The biggest risk is *not* taking one." I saw that quote in a magazine for an insurance company, and I thought it was a very clever ad. An insurance company advertising the idea that risks are necessary for achieving your goals seemed like the antithesis of a typical insurance company's philosophy. Robert Kiyosaki said almost the same thing in *Rich Dad, Poor Dad*: "In today's rapidly changing world, the people who are not taking risk are the risk takers."

A universal trait of successful people is that they take risks. I take risks every day. Most people wouldn't even consider the risks that I take in order to grow my business. I have maxed out all of my credit cards, closed out my 401k several times, borrowed millions of dollars that I personally guarantee, and put everything I own on the line several times. Taking risks in your personal life and business, if well thought out, will always lead to success at some point. It is important to remember that the risks you take must be morally, legally, and ethically correct.

Taking the frozen shot risk was a big one, but I knew if I were to suffer a few setbacks I could recover and try again. If Zeus Juice had not suffered the temporary defeat as a result of my risk-taking, I would not have found my first job in the business I am in now. I would not have made millions in this business, and I certainly would not be writing this book.

Taking a risk is absolutely necessary to be successful in business and your personal life. When analyzing the risk, apply the 3 P's + 1 P technique, and you will minimize the potential for your risk-taking to cause financial or emotional distress. 3 P's + 1 P will also alleviate any fear that you may have. Fear is a biomarker of excusetosis, and can impede your ability to take calculated risks. Successful people take risks!

Bill Gates was quoted as saying, "To win big, you sometimes have to take big risks." Donald Trump, Michael Dell, Steve Jobs, and everyone before them *all* took risks. All of them also use and apply several of the strategies and techniques in my book. Just ask any successful person you know, and they will tell you they take risks.

Here are the stories of a few famous and successful risk-takers:

STEVE JOBS, FOUNDER OF APPLE AND PIXAR

Steve Jobs dropped out of Reed College after a semester, spent a year in India, and returned to found Apple with his friend, Stephen Wozniak.

Mr. Jobs was forced out of Apple in 1985, went off and founded two other companies, NeXT and Pixar, before returning to Apple in 1996 and becoming chief executive officer in 1997. NeXT did not work, but Mr. Jobs put practically every dollar he had into Pixar, and that risk paid off, big-time.

TIM WESTERGREN, FOUNDER OF PANDORA RADIO

In the winter of 2001, Pandora was completely out of money. Tim Westergren had a clear choice: cut his losses or find a way to make it work. He decided to keep the company alive by deferring salaries—risks that employees took. Ultimately, more than fifty people deferred roughly $1.5 million over the course of two years. In 2004, with eleven of his credit cards maxed out, they got an infusion of cash, and the rest is history.

JERRY JONES, OWNER OF THE DALLAS COWBOYS

In 1989, when the Dallas Cowboys franchise was losing $1 million a month and was nowhere near "America's Team," Jerry Jones bought 13 percent of the franchise for close to $155 million. He spent nearly everything he had. In 2008, he broke ground on one of the most ambitious stadium builds in the history of the NFL, and now the Dallas Cowboys are valued at close to $2 billion dollars!

DAVID CHOE, FAMOUS ARTIST

Although not at risk of living in the street if it didn't pay off, David Choe, a famous contemporary muralist, was asked by Sean Parker, then president of a little-known company called Facebook, to paint their offices for free in exchange for stock options. Choe would normally have charged $60,000 to paint his famous murals on the office walls, but agreed to do it for stock. Now Choe's risk has paid off to the tune of about $200 million in stock value.

CURTIS JAMES JACKSON, AKA 50 CENT, FAMOUS RAPPER/ENTERTAINER

Now, 50 Cent did not live the most righteous life in his earlier years, but he took a risk that some rumored to be worth over $400 million when he was asked by Vitamin Water to be their spokesperson and appear in their advertisements. He agreed, but took the risk—betting his time and potential royalty deal—of opting for stock instead of a royalty. According to my research, after all was said and done, 50 Cent walked away with close to $100 million.

The key to taking risks is to minimize that risk by being prepared and thinking through every possible scenario. Taking risks also involves vision, an intangible part of taking a risk that cannot be put on paper or into a formula. Sometimes you have to trust your vision and instinct.

STAND UP—AND BE YOURSELF

Asking for more isn't *only* about material things or money; it's also about how you feel at the end of the day. Ask yourself: Are you able to have a hobby? Do you do things that just make you happy? I am not a very religious person, but I believe in my own inner spirit and the inner spirit of all human beings. If your inner spirit is not happy, then happiness will be very difficult to find. Many times the self-fulfilling prophecy that comes your way is a direct result of your inner thoughts, emotions, and spirit. Be happy and you will find happiness; be miserable and you will find misery. It's tough to be happy when you are surrounded by despair, but there is always a silver lining to everything, and once you find it, you will find happiness.

I always thought I was a funny guy. I enjoy stand-up comedy, and one day I was discussing my hysterical comedic talent with a friend and he challenged me to get on stage and see if a bunch of strangers agreed with my assessment of my humor. Well, I took that challenge, and I wouldn't say that I "killed it" (comedians' expression for doing very well) but I had a good set. That was several months ago, and I have continued to go up on stage. I have performed in Boston, Los Angeles, Orlando, and San Diego at some pretty major comedy clubs. They were all open mics, but some were very difficult to actually get stage time in, such as the iconic Improv in Hollywood. As I continued to do stand-up, the very friend who challenged me asked to take me out to lunch, which doesn't happen that often. He sat me down and said, "Mike, you have a very successful company, you are on TV every day with some of the top-rated infomercials, you are a successful lawyer, you have a book deal . . . what's up with the comedy? Are you having a midlife crisis? What is your endgame?"

I told him I didn't have an endgame, and I'm not having a midlife crisis. I told him, "I just want to be happy. I had a goal of performing at a club in Boston to see if the crowd responded, which they did, but I have no endgame." Sometimes you do things just for fun; stand-up comedy for me is just a hobby. I actually enjoy the art of comedy and how one word, one facial expression, or your tone of voice can make or break a joke. Not everything you do has to have an endgame.

KYLA CAN DO NO WRONG

I had a dog named Kyla for almost ten years. We adopted her at the local shelter, and she was the best dog anyone could wish for. She was a big, intimidating-looking dog when we saw her, and she was probably about five years old. She sat in the pound for several months with an eye infection, a skin infection, and generally looking pretty scary. We think she was part pit bull and part pointer. That combination of being tall with a big chest, a big head, and all muscle made her difficult to want to adopt. Kyla was loyal, yet mischievous, a beggar but also a listener, strong but gentle: all in all, an amazing dog. We adopted her for $100 but spent roughly $8,000 on having both knees fixed, and we loved this dog like a blood relative.

Kyla grew old and began to lose her senses and faculties. It was so sad to see, because she also seemed happy. Eventually her breathing became so labored that we were concerned she would have a heart attack. After consulting with the veterinarian, we made one of the most gut-wrenching decisions: it was time to put her down. We actually scheduled a date, one that no dog lover is ever prepared for. But before that date, for about a week, we had a Kyla Could

Do No Wrong policy and treated her like the queen she was. We gave her steak for dinner and marrow bones all day long. She slept where she wanted and did what she wanted. We spent as much time petting her and loving her as possible. We bought her special dog treats and she got tons of them. Her last day, she happily sat on our front lawn and chewed on a marrow bone. On the way to the veterinarian's I stopped and got her a bagel with peanut butter. When we arrived at the veterinarian's office I brought with me a cushion from the couch she loved. And then she peacefully went to dog heaven. I loved that dog!

But, the point of telling you this story is that sometimes you too have to have a *You* Can Do No Wrong Day and live life. Enjoy the things that make you happy, spend time with your family. Do whatever makes you happy. I'm still figuring life out, but after having a Kyla Can Do No Wrong Week, it dawned on me that we need the same thing, not when it is our time to go, but whenever we can. It is good for the soul. You always hear people who have beat cancer have more of an appreciation for life, for the smaller things like actually smelling the roses and the coffee. So in your pursuit of success, whatever that may be, on your way there and when you get there, make sure you have a *You* Can Do No Wrong Day here and there. I am very fortunate to be able to have several Do No Wrong Days in a row.

It's also a good idea to give someone you know a *You* Can Do No Wrong Day, whether it be a spouse, sibling, or coworker; everyone needs one. If you feel like a day is not possible, you can do an hour, a half-day, or whatever it is. Ask yourself: When was the last time I had a Do No Wrong Day?

DON'T FIGHT AUTHORITY: RESPECT IT AND DEMAND THAT IT RESPECT YOU!

As a kid I obviously had drive and wanted more, but I also partici-pated in activities that no one would be proud of. Shoplifting was an option for me as a kid. I never got caught, and to be honest it wasn't something I did a lot, but I did. One time I was at the mall with two of my friends and we were in Sears. As we walked out we were approached by an undercover security guard. Both of my friends had stolen video games; I for some reason, thankfully did not! Even though I hadn't stolen anything, we were all brought to the security area, and we had to call our parents and were told we were never allowed in the store again. I was "scared straight," as they would say.

When people ask me what made me different than a lot of the kids I grew up with, I joke around and say, "Well, I never got caught." But, what really set me apart was that I respected authority and my elders. I was deathly afraid of getting in trouble; I was already the poor kid, and people expected me to be involved in petty crime, but I just didn't want to make it any worse. Many of the kids that I grew up with just didn't care. They were already fatally infected with excuse-tosis and ultimately had no self-respect. I wanted more than to be accepted by my peers and their parents; I wanted to be respected. In order to be respected you have to respect others. I think my mom told me that.

HOW I LEARNED TO STOP BEING AFRAID TO OFFEND: THE POWER OF "FUCK"

I never imagined that my book would use expletives, and I had a hard time recognizing the benefit of using what some may find an offensive word in my book. But, well, I grew up just outside of Boston, and the word "fuck" is just a part of our everyday vernacular. It is not a word you want to use around children, and it is obviously offensive to some. However, the offensiveness of the word is what also makes it powerful. It is not appropriate in every situation, but when used properly it can be *very* effective.

Case in point: about a year ago, I had an employee who works for me mess up a major part of her job. She has a very important position, and the information she gives to me affects my business decisions as well as the entire company and its employees. This person also is a very good friend of mine and she has known me since I was twelve. All this meant that she ended up becoming the unfortunate (or I could say fortunate) person to learn about the power of "fuck."

The conversation went something like this:

Me: Sue, you realize that you *fucked* up royally? You realize that because you were not prepared and essentially didn't do your job, that you *fucked* me and the company, right?

Sue: Michael, why are you talking like this to me? Why are you degrading me?

Me: Sue, you have known me since I was twelve, right?

Sue: Yeah.

Me: Have I not used the word "fuck" since then?

Sue: Yeah.

Me: Okay, then, well you fucked up, almost cost me and the company *millions*, and you almost got fired. Don't ever do it again, and remember this conversation in the future. I still love you.

Now, there are many businesspeople who would totally disagree with the use of this word. They would say that I am immature, that there are more effective ways to communicate, and it is just down-right crass. Well, they may be right. But, I know this: Sue has never made the mistake again, and as a result she double- and triple-checks her data before giving it to me. I also challenge her, and for the most part, her information since the above conversation has been correct.

Did I offend her? Yeah, probably. Did she get it? Did she understand the magnitude of her mistake? Yes, she did. Will she make the same mistake again? Well, I don't have a crystal ball in front of me. But, by my "offending" her by using the word *fuck*, she got it.

I actually held a meeting about being more assertive and, yes, using the word *fuck* with my executives. Most of my day consists of speaking with my executives about the business and our vendors, clients, and customers. Many times I give a directive, and because it is not in the executives' demeanor, they are not as aggressive as they should be and thus not as effective. I had a call center that takes a lot of our calls essentially steal from our company, treat my customers poorly, and ultimately just do a horrible job. I asked one of my executives to express my concerns and to fix it. Well, as I bet you can guess, the executive was not as passionate with his concerns and was a little more "professional." But, I have to point out that we have a very large staff, and they have families and children. They depend on us. Furthermore, we have customers who expect a certain level of service, and our reputation is everything. When a vendor does not do what we expect on our behalf, they are essentially telling me, my employees, and my customers to *fuck off*, and I am extremely offended by such a lack of care and service. I picked up the phone and expressed my concerns to the VP of sales and marketing at this particular call center, using the word *fuck* as a verb, an adjective, and a noun, and guess what? They fixed the problem and gave us a credit.

One time I picked up the phone and said to a vendor, "I know you are fucking me." That's all I said. The vendor responded and *asked me* what I wanted. As you already know, when I said that I knew what I wanted. They had about $250,000 of my money (they are essentially a bank), and I wanted it, now. Guess what? I got it, *and* they reduced the rate that they were charging me in the future.

Now, if you do not use this word in your life and you are offended by it, then let me apologize. It is not the use of the word *fuck* that is important. It is the use of the English language in a way that will effectively convey to the other party that they have screwed you, hurt you, or disappointed you. And, you cannot be afraid to offend someone who *fucks* you, in your personal or business life, because at the end of the day you are the only one who is responsible for making YOU Enterprises, Inc. successful.

RELATIONSHIPS

One thing I have learned in my thirty-eight years on this planet is the importance of developing and maintaining strong personal and business relationships. When the time comes to *ask* for *more* from people, they are much more receptive if you have a relationship with them. In business I have developed strong relationships that have grown and become stronger over time. Many of these relationships truly were built on a handshake and my word. I'm sure you always hear things like "my word is my bond," or "you have my word." But, if you don't really mean it, if you don't stick to what you agreed to, then your word is worthless.

As business relationships develop and even evolve into friendships, your professional life will thrive and grow. When I first got into the direct response industry I was at a free cocktail party with a colleague. I was what some people would call "green." I didn't know anyone, and we were there to network. A man walked up to my colleague and me and introduced himself. We didn't know him or anything about the company he worked for. That relationship began on a handshake, and my good friend Mark Biglow, a partner at Mercury Media, has gone to bat for me several times. His company financed many of my projects based on my word, and as I type, I still owe them money, but we continue to do business and pay down our balances. This relationship, which was built on a handshake and a word, has literally generated tens of millions of dollars. I have *asked* them for things most people would not even consider asking, but because of our relationship, not only did they grant my requests, but they continue to.

When I first started Blue Vase I had limited funds, credit cards, and my word. My credit cards and limited funds alone would not have gotten me to where I am today. Since I am in the advertising business, our biggest expense is media. When you buy media you have to pay two weeks in advance. I did not have two weeks' worth of media to grow my company. But I had developed a relationship with a man by the name of Peter Bieler. Peter is one of the most successful people in the direct response industry; he has a beautiful house in the hills of Malibu and was responsible for the Thigh Master infomercial. As a result of our strong relationship, Peter has literally loaned me tens of millions of dollars. A kid from the projects with no ties to wealthy people was able to take the only thing I had—the only thing you have—my *word*, to grow my business.

About three years ago, my business was growing at a rapid pace. We had close to two hundred people and we were doing millions of dollars in sales every week. My accountant, who was new to the industry, had made some miscalculations, and we were actually hemorrhaging money. Yes, I realize that last sentence sounds a whole lot like an excuse, and I am really the one responsible, but for purposes of the story that's what happened. But by the time I realized what had really happened, we owed Peter over $1 million, and I had nothing in our bank account. I needed another $250,000 just to cover payroll. I will never forget that day. I was actually sitting on a park bench talking with some of my executives and trying to solve this enormous challenge. The only person I knew who could lend that kind of money on a *handshake* was Peter, the guy I already owed all the money to that I couldn't pay back!

I called him up, explained the situation and *asked* him to wire me $250,000! Well, he didn't just immediately say yes; he actually had to look at a lot of things, speak with his team, and make a major decision. His numbers showed that we were not looking good financially, and he was concerned about the original million that I owed him. We spoke for about an hour, and he asked me to come up with a plan for how I was going to pay him back. In about an hour we developed a plan, which involved having to lay people off, reduce our media, and take a long, hard look at our expenses. We sent him the report, and after a little more discussion he agreed.

Ultimately, what allowed Peter to do this was our strong relationship and my word. To this day, Peter is a financing partner on several of my television campaigns, and I consider him a good friend.

Ask yourself: Is your *word* really your *word*? How strong are your relationships? What makes your relationships stronger? Your *word*.

IS THAT HOW YOU WANT TO BE REMEMBERED?— REVISITED

I was recently talking with a former eighth grade teacher about life. I told him that if it weren't for some teachers giving me the *opportunity* to change my ways by giving me more *responsibility*, then I probably would have ended up dead, in jail, or addicted to drugs. He told me about an exercise that he had all of his eighth grade students do at the end of the school year: he had them write their own obituary. He said he started doing this in 1968 in inner-city Los Angeles. In 1968, we had the LA riots, the country was in complete turmoil over the Vietnam War, racial tensions were extremely high, and LA was just a scary place to live. So he figured this might help make the kids look forward to a better time in their lives. He didn't give me any compelling, tear-jerking story, but he did tell me about one student who wrote in his obituary that he "was" the head football coach. Well, that kid actually became the head football coach and went on to become the principal of a neighboring high school.

What would your obituary look like *right now*? What would people write about you? Have you ever read the obituary section and seen an entry that just states the person's name and date of death? Why do you think that is? Who were these people? What did they do in life? What was their legacy? Wasn't there more to say? Maybe there was not because they didn't *ask* for *more* in their life.

What will your obituary read when you ultimately pass? I didn't realize this, but I have been asking myself that question a lot during my life, just not in those exact words. I constantly ask myself, "What will my legacy be?" But, I also ask myself, "What do I *want* it to be?" The good news is, right *now* you can control what your legacy will be and how your obituary will read.

I don't ask in this book that you do many activities. But do this: write your own obituary. It is very difficult to do and seems a bit morbid. But do it and see how you feel. Write it as of today. If you are not happy with what is on that piece of paper, then you can change it. You have time.

CHAPTER 9

WHAT GOES AROUND STARTS WITH YOU: GIVE BACK!

Most of the rich, famous, and super successful people I have known give back, whether through donations, setting up charitable foundations, or donating their actual time. But you don't have to be rich and famous to give back; that's just what good human beings do.

When I was in high school we had a program that recognized students for things such as picking up trash at the high school to donating their time at the local food pantry. The program was called Beverly High Pride. When students did something, other students would nominate their peers for a Pride Pin. It was a real honor to get a Pride Pin. One cold winter day we were on a field trip in Boston, and we were having lunch at a pizza place. When we were all done eating we realized that we had enough pizza to feed at least a dozen more people. I came up with the idea to find some homeless people and give them this warm, fresh, and awesome pizza. We walked around and found a group of homeless men battling the cold, sur-rounding a barrel with a controlled fire in it, trying to stay warm. A group of us walked up to them and handed them a few large pizzas. I don't remember what was said, but I will never forget the look in one of the men's eyes, a look of absolute appreciation and thanks. It warmed my heart, and the feeling that I got is indescribable.

Zig Ziglar says you have not helped people until you help some-one who cannot repay the favor. In high school I didn't know who Zig Ziglar was, but he is right. Helping those in need without any sort of expectation of a return favor will change you and give you an appreciation for what you have. To end this story, I was nominated for a Pride Pin along with a few of my peers, and I was extremely proud, but that was secondary to the amazing feeling I had sharing with someone who couldn't pay me back.

That feeling may have been enhanced by the fact that more than a few times during my youth I was on the other side of the equation and knew what it felt like to have someone else care. You see, when my mother was diagnosed with HIV, it was devastating to me, and back then it was a death sentence. My mom never made a lot of money in her life but was always a hard worker, and she is just a gra-cious, generous person. When she realized that she had this disease, there were a few organizations that she reached out to, and they helped us with things such as rent, Christmas gifts, car payments, and other daily expenses. The name of the organization was called Aids Action North Shore. It is an amazing group of people who help sufferers cope with this disease.

But even as my mother was battling her own pain and suffering, she gave back in a way that cannot be valued or quantified, and it impacted me greatly. When I was in high school, no one knew about my mother's diagnosis, but she *asked* how she could help Aids Action. Aids Action asked her to speak at high schools and tell her story. I never went to one of her speeches and she never spoke at my high school, due to the stigma it may have caused for me. One day my mother came home and told me how she spoke at Hamilton Wenham High School in a neighboring town. After her speech a young man came up to her, thanked her, and hugged her. Well, that young man also knew me and my friends very well. My mother was fearful that he would tell others about her status and somehow hurt me. He never did, but I decided that since my mother was okay with telling her story, educating people and giving back, that I was also okay with it.

Her story likely saved people's lives. I know that a major part of her story was safe sex. My mom was not a drug addict but was infected by my stepfather. Absolutely devastating! But, through her speeches I am sure high school kids who were having sex protected themselves and potentially saved their own lives.

Now giving back does not always have to pull at the heartstrings. Random acts of kindness are also a great way to give back. Last year I was lost just outside of Orlando, and I kept looping around and going through the same tollbooth. Well, I finally ran out of quarters at the tollbooth. In Orlando many of these tollbooths are unmanned. I didn't know what to do when I looked back and realized there was a car behind me. I decided to get out of my car and ask a random man behind me for a dollar. Orlando, like many major cities, has some major crime, and Florida has many citizens who carry firearms. But I only had two options: blow through the booth or ask for help. The man in a beat-up old Honda Accord handed me four quarters without thinking. Now this is only *one dollar*, but I was so grateful. I'm not sure if he had the same feeling, but it made me feel great that I was able to ask a fellow human being for help.

GOING TO THE AMUSEMENT PARK

When I was a kid, my dad's employer used to have a family day at a local amusement park. They would pay for the day, food, and rides. I remember being so excited. A young, poor kid doesn't get to go to amusement parks all that often. It was such a treat. A few years later there was a local youth center in my town who used to have counselors go to the local neighborhoods and talk to kids like me; they used to sponsor events that took kids to the same amusement park my dad's work brought me to. I was fortunate enough to be able to go to the park with the youth center and some of my neighborhood friends, and again, it was such a fun time. We were able to get out of the neighborhood for a day and just enjoy the innocence of being a kid.

Recently, as a part of my community outreach program for Blue Vase, we organized a trip to the exact same park for more than thirty underprivileged kids plus a parent. We are paying for transportation on a nice bus, food for the day, all-access passes to the rides, plus ten dollars a kid. Why am I doing this? The times that I was fortunate enough to be able to get out of my neighborhood and just be a kid helped change my life. If I can do the same for those kids, then my legacy will go beyond what I could possibly imagine. I may never know if this fun day helps change these kids' lives, but it makes me feel that I am contributing to the greater good of humanity. I do this because someone did it for me. People always talk about the concept of karma and how your actions, good or bad, come back to you some way. It is a fact and relates to what I previously touched upon: your inner spirit. When you do good things, your inner spirit will be happy and your outer world will also be good to you. Karma is a real thing, and most people don't think about its power, but what you do today will affect you tomorrow.

ARCADE OR CASINO?

Giving back doesn't necessarily involve a charitable event. Give back to your friends or family. Giving back doesn't necessarily involve money, either. If you can help someone with a challenging situation, then you should. I'm a lawyer, so most friends and family think I know everything about the law. That is not the case for any lawyer. However, when a legal challenge arrives and I am asked to help, I help as best as I can.

About seven years ago a very good friend of mine opened up an arcade. But the arcade was very unique: his arcade had machines that looked like slot machines and video poker. But, they were not machines that paid out cash. Their system was exactly what Chuck E. Cheese's does: you play a game, win tickets, and redeem them for a prize. About a year after he opened with all of the proper approvals and licenses, he was shut down by the town. There were accusations that he was running an illegal casino, but we all knew he wasn't. He came to me and asked me to help. I knew nothing about gaming law, but I knew I could find someone who did. After several hours of research and reaching out to my network of lawyer friends, I found a few experts in the field who were able to successfully argue to the town and the commonwealth that what my friend was doing was legal and was not a casino. As a result he was able to open back up. That was seven years ago. As I type today, the laws have changed and my friend opened a second arcade, but about a week ago both places were raided and shut down by the attorney general, and it is now a criminal matter. I am not a criminal lawyer, but I have begun to help mount his defense. Giving back to friends, family, and even strangers is what makes the world go round. If you can help, then you should. It's that simple.

A LITTLE GIRL GOES TO CAMP

When I was a kid, my mother found a way to get me to go to camp during the summer. Sometimes it was a week, other times it was a whole month. The camp was sponsored by the YMCA and was one of the best things for me. Every morning I was picked up by a bus and went to the YMCA campus to spend all day doing things like playing sports, swimming, arts and crafts, going on adventure walks, and playing with other kids. When I think about this time, I am very grateful for what my mother was able to accomplish, and it was truly a wonderful experience. I was able to get out of the neighborhood, see new things, meet new people, and be a kid.

When I graduated from high school, I went to Springfield College in Springfield, Massachusetts, the birthplace of American basketball and also a school that was founded on the principles of Spirit, Mind, and Body. One of the college's main missions was to help promote churches and the YMCA. I didn't pick Springfield for this reason, but it seems that the YMCA and I have been connected since my childhood.

Since I was so fond of my time at the YMCA summer camp, I wanted to give less-fortunate kids the ability to go to have similar experiences. It seemed like a nice thing to do, but it became a difficult task due to the red tape of the YMCA. I had my human resources manager reach out to the YMCA to tell them that we wanted to send a few kids to camp for the summer. But again, due to the red tape, it couldn't be done. We were told to just make a donation, but I wanted to do more. I wanted to make sure an underprivileged child was going to be able to go to camp with our donation. Not just a general cash donation, but one with a purpose and that was dear to my heart. Well, you should know by now that I don't accept "it can't be done" for an answer.

Early in the summer of 2011, I went for a walk outside my office, which also happens to be located behind my old neighborhood. I went for this walk so that I could walk through my old neighborhood to find some kids in need and offer to send them to camp. Now, I must say this seems a little odd—a big guy in shorts and a T-shirt, perspiring a bit, walking through my old neighborhood, looking to send kids to camp.

The actual house that I grew up in had a little girl the same age as my daughter playing out front by herself. She was a cute little girl, and I thought she would be a perfect candidate. So I stood on the corner waiting for her mom to come out so I could approach her and tell her what I wanted to do. It seemed like an eternity standing there, and I felt a little uneasy. Finally, her mother, Maria, did come out, and I approached her and told her what I wanted to do. Of course she was a little guarded and skeptical, but we talked at length and I asked her to meet me in my office the upcoming Monday. Maria arrived at my office on that Monday, and she was a little taken aback. I remember she said, "You are real," and I didn't really understand what she meant. She went on to say that the situation in which I approached her on a Saturday afternoon—randomly, in shorts, unshaven, and perspiring a bit—just didn't seem real. I have to admit she had every right to be skeptical.

After cutting through the red tape at the YMCA, we were able to send her daughter to camp for the summer. When I think about this, it warms my heart. Maria and her daughter were very grateful and appreciative of my generosity. But, I was more appreciative to be able to give back to a young child what was given to me as a kid. Those summers when my mother was able to get a grant or come up with the money to send me to camp had a lasting impression on my life. I wanted to and will continue to give back as so many others gave to me.

By the way, Maria was unemployed when I spoke with her. She was intelligent, had worked for the airlines for several years, and had fallen on hard times. I asked her to send me her résumé, and told her I might have a position for her. Even though I am a generous person and believe in the power of giving back, I will not give people jobs solely for the purpose of employing them. However, Maria had skills that were an asset to my company. She now works for Blue Vase Marketing in our quality control department and has added tremendous value to that department.

Think about what really happened in the above story. I wanted to give something back with no intention of getting something in return, other than the warm feeling and pride of being able to help others in need. What really happened? My generosity *instantly* gave me back something of value. I now have a very professional, very caring, and hardworking employee who continues to add value to my company.

Benevolent intentions are not benevolent if you are hoping for something in return, but if your heart is in the right place, it always comes back one way or another.

STAND UP FOR A FRIEND

One night after one of my comedy routines I was talking with a couple of local comedians who were actually from the same town I am from. We got to discussing sports and then football. One of the comedians, Jeff Koen (star of the movie *Heavy Times*), and I both played linebacker together. The other comedian, Dave Rattigan, is a writer for a few Boston newspapers, host of a sports talk radio show, and has been on Sirius XM a lot. One of us mentioned a friend who also played linebacker, Eric Shairs. Eric was paralyzed in a tragic pool accident about ten years ago. He dove into the pool, hit his head, and then climbed out of the pool, but that movement severed his spinal column, and he is now a quadriplegic. He has two girls and tragically, this accident actually happened in front of them. Eric is a great guy, and he was a physical specimen and an unbelievable athlete as well. So Dave, Jeff, and myself came up with the idea of doing a comedy night to help raise some funds for Eric. His expenses are extraordinary and insurance doesn't cover a lot of them. So, I spearheaded the organization of this event and we had an amazing night. Dave, Jeff, myself, and two other comedians, Chris Dimitrakopoulos (Chris D) and Juston McKinney (*The Tonight Show*, Comedy Central), all killed it and essentially donated our services. We raised a lot of money, but most important, everyone laughed. Eric had an amazing time. Now, Eric and I were not super close when we played together. But we did this event because Eric is a great guy, because Jeff, Dave, and I all live in the same town as Eric, and because it was just the right and fun thing to do.

By the way, Eric is also truly an inspiration. He went from being an amazing athlete to being confined to a chair, and likely could be that way for the rest of his life (though I hope modern science will prove us wrong). He has limited mobility of his arms and hands, and as a result he was able to have his car retrofitted so he can actually drive with his hands! Yet Eric went on to get his master's and works at a local college, helping students pick their classes and keeping them on the right track. He is a very positive person who wakes up every day, takes his daughters to their softball games, goes to the beach, goes to physical therapy, and tries to live a normal life. He also believes that someday he will walk again. I believe that with modern science and a little help from friends, family, and even strangers, that goal will be accomplished.

If you would like to help Eric achieve his goal, you could send a check to The Eric Shairs Recovery Fund, 100 Cummings Center, Suite 354B, Beverly, MA 01915.

BOOTSTRAPPING

As I mention in the advertisement for my book, and earlier in the book itself, I grew up poor. I was the beneficiary of many government and nongovernment programs on the local, state, and federal levels. One in particular is a small charitable organization called Beverly Bootstraps. This is a very unique charitable organization that offers a wide variety of services for people in need. But when I was a kid, my mother used to go to them to get things like food and even help with the rent, utilities, and other necessities. Since my company is based in Beverly, Massachusetts, where I grew up, I felt compelled to give back to the local community, the one that had the most impact on my life. I didn't do this out of feelings of guilt, but as a part of my duty as a human being and a citizen of this country.

Since I have opened my doors, we have done some pretty remarkable things that I am proud of. We held a diaper drive that provided families with things like diapers, sanitary napkins, soap, and other things most people take for granted. We held an Easter basket drive for local families so that their children could enjoy the fun part of the Easter holiday. Imagine what that little kid felt like when he or she came downstairs and the Easter Bunny came. That has to warm your heart. We also have done the traditional Toys for Tots programs and food drives. One year, we actually sponsored individual families and took care of their entire Christmas celebrations!

You won't meet a truly successful person who doesn't give back in one way or another. Giving back is, in my opinion, your inherent social responsibility. Some may claim that there are many people milking the system, and that may be true, but there are many individuals who are not; they are simply hardworking people trying to get by. Pick a charitable organization that is dear to your heart, and get active: check out a local animal shelter or the United Way. It doesn't matter, as you will get so much in return. But you will also appreciate what you have. I am not a socialist and don't believe in coddling people, but I do believe that we, as a human race, since the beginning of time have helped each other get to where we are today. Everyone needs a little help sometimes—even *me*!

Giving back doesn't need to have a charitable aspect to it. Give back to your friends, your family, and your community. What I mean is, help people out when you can. If someone needs help in moving, if someone is having trouble with a car, or whatever it is, help out. I am a very busy person, but I am always available to help my friends, neighbors, relatives, or business associates. Someday, sometime, you will need help, and people remember what you did for them. By helping someone now, you are essentially *asking* them to help you later, without actually asking.

This is not the end of *Ask More, Get More*. The next section has additional powerful techniques, secrets, and strategies that will get you more out of life. So, get ready—because people asked me for more.

VACATION FOR FREE?

Yes, it is possible and can be accomplished many ways. I have a little girl who has been fortunate enough to visit Disney World a couple of times. The last time we went for two weeks, the first week was *free*! That's right—*free*! How is this possible? Well, I have a credit card where I earn points, known as Disney Points, that I can use toward any hotel on the Disney World properties. I also have traveled all over the United States, from Miami to Santa Monica, for *free*!

Earlier we discussed credit cards and how to use them properly. One of the things that I recommend is using credit cards that give cash back and allow you to earn points. American Express allows you to earn points which you can basically use for anything you want. They offer a $200 credit each year that can be used on

JetBlue, though you have to make sure that you actually use it. A friend of mine traveled to China and back *first class* by using his AMEX points. That is equivalent to a $17,000 plane ticket. Find a credit card that offers cash back, points, or other incentives that allow you to use them for whatever you want. Debit cards also have incentives, depending on the bank. You can go to my website at www.AskMore-GetMore.com for a list of credit cards that offer all types of incentives.

Many of us have heard the term "frequent flyer miles." I have friends who have enough frequent flyer miles to travel almost every day for ten years and not run out. Many times if you travel for work, you can personally accumulate the frequent flyer miles and use them for your family vacation. The best way to do this is to pick a particular airline, and if possible, only use that airline when you travel. There are alliances among airlines. For instance, the Star Alliance is Continental, United, US Airways, Air Canada, Lufthansa, and several other airlines; traveling on any of these airlines will allow you to aggregate frequent flyer miles.

TIP: Points.com is a cool website that allows you to trade different types of points with others to get what you are looking for: bartering at its best.

SPEND A DAY GETTING PITCHED AND TRAVEL FOR FREE!

I first learned of this technique when I was a young child, and I was able to go to Disney World with my mom. I wondered how we were able to travel with hardly any money. Now my mom did essentially spend her tax refund money on the trip, but a large portion of the trip was taken care of by a company that lured us down to Florida to pitch us time-shares. That was pretty funny, since we could barely buy milk, but we were showed several properties that were available for a time-share or purchase. I remember being bored, but it paid for a good portion of my Disney adventure. We had our hotel and even passes to Disney World paid for just by spending a couple of hours looking at things we couldn't afford. These types of programs are offered every day, all over the country. Some are better than others, but they are a great way to travel for *free*! On my website I list many companies that offer *free* vacations just to convince people to hear what they have to say.

START A BUSINESS AND TRAVEL AROUND THE WORLD FOR *FREE*!

I know people who have started and own travel agencies for the sole purpose of traveling for free. When you own a travel agency, you will find that hotels and resorts want you to come to their property so that you can recommend them to your prospective clients. Some of the people I know travel to five-star hotels where they are catered to hand and foot for weeks on end, and the entire trip, including airfare, is paid for! Some of these resorts will also pay for the family to come along with the agent. This is a great technique and easy to use.

There are also several home-based businesses that tap into the multitrillion-dollar travel industry, thus creating travel agents that make money based on a multilevel marketing plan. Many of them have created and continue to create millionaires. Multilevel marketing companies get a bad reputation for many reasons, but companies like Amway, Herbalife, Shaklee, Melaleuca, and YTB Travel are multimillion-dollar, multinational companies that do give people financial freedom. On my website I list several home-based businesses that tap into the travel industry, and you can decide for yourself.

Also, if you have a business and you need to travel for your business, you can write off essentially every expense that is related to your business. If you need to go to France, China, or South Africa for your business you are entitled to write these expenses off. Let's face it; you don't spend every waking hour working when you travel. I call these working vacations and they are great. You can accomplish your business goals and objectives, but you can also vacation.

BECOME A MYSTERY SHOPPER

I have a friend whose dad has not paid to go out to eat in over three years. He is retired, so to keep busy he works as a mystery shopper. He is even a mystery shopper for local restaurants that serve items like pizza and Chinese food. He does simple things like take a picture of the food when it arrives at his house and details whether the driver was on time and courteous. He must also note if he was offered specials and checks to make sure they delivered the order correctly, among other things. These are all things that you do anyway—so why not get paid to do it, and eat for *free*?

There are organizations that serve the travel and hospitality industry by providing mystery shoppers to give evaluations of the industry. So, you could travel for free and enjoy the nicest hotels, spas, and cruises in the world just by becoming a mystery shopper.

There are companies that will hire you as a consultant to go to a really nice hotel—let's say the Ritz Carlton in Miami. You go for *free*, stay for *free*, go to the spa, eat at their restaurants, order room service, and everything in between, *and* you get paid for it! This is real! On my website I have links to companies such as the Coyle Hospitality Group, which has been providing mystery shoppers for the hospitality industry since 1966, and you could be one of their next shoppers!

HOUSE SWAP

This is one of my favorites. You can go stay at homes all over the world for *free*! All you have to do is give up your home for the same amount of time. This is a great way to see different parts of the world without having to pay for your stay. A friend of mine does this all the time by following this process: He accumulates

ASK MORE, GET MORE

frequent flyer mile points so that he can fly anywhere in the continental United States for free and makes sure he has enough miles for his wife and two kids. He then swaps his home with families from all over the country. When this happens, he usually gets to use that family's car, their Internet, and their phone—he is literally trading spaces with another family for a certain period of time. There are a bunch of online agencies that allow you to swap houses with other families in exchange for a small fee, or you can go on Craigslist and do it for *free* on your own. I have a list of many of these agencies on AskMore-GetMore.com.

GET GROCERIES FOR *FREE*!

Getting groceries for free is simple, and *anyone* can do this—you don't need a computer, a credit card, or anything else. All you need is a little bit of time and persistence. The term "couponing," or "extreme couponing," has become popular due to certain reality shows, which feature soccer moms who seem to get high by saving money and getting their groceries for *free*. I can't blame them. The average household spends between $140 and $280 a week on groceries. On the high end, that is a savings of $15,000 a year! Now, take that $15k and put it in the stock market, and guess what that turns into in fifty years? $4,335,032.85—that is the power of compound interest. *Four million, three hundred thousand dollars!* I have a compound interest calculator on my website, AskMore-GetMore.com, so you can play with the numbers.

But in a nutshell, extreme couponing involves dedicating time toward acquiring as many coupons as possible. At first glance, this may seem like an all-consuming task. In fact, it is easy to unearth a number of cost-effective and time-efficient couponing tips that can put hundreds of dollars back into your wallet. Not only do these techniques save money, they are also user-friendly, as these methods are easy enough for even the most casual shopper to reap noticeable results. Here is a list of some of these tips.

Subscribe to the Sunday Paper. Let's start with something easy: a subscription to a reputable Sunday paper instantly brings you access to a plethora of coupons for a variety of products. If you can't afford a subscription, go to local stores that carry the Sunday paper, and at the end of the day ask for the coupons. You can go to multiple stores and get hundreds of coupons this way.

Don't Rush. Spending just fifteen minutes of coupon clipping won't get you groceries for free, but will certainly save you a lot of money. However, like anything else in life, the amount of success you experience with couponing depends on the amount of effort you put into it. Try and get as much information as possible about the sales and coupons offered by your favorite grocery stores, and then plan accordingly. Thanks to the Internet, this has become easy.

Learn the Coupon Policies of Your Local Stores. Some grocers offer triple- or double-coupon days. This means that they will either double or triple the savings that the coupon offers. For example, suppose you bring in a coupon for $1 off on crackers. On double coupon day, you will actually receive $2 off your purchase. This policy is not without restrictions; stores usually only offer to double coupons up to a certain amount, typically around the one-dollar mark, and sometimes they limit the number of coupons you are allowed to double. Local grocers may also allow you to use coupons from other stores, or to "stack" coupons. "Stacking" occurs when a shopper stocks up on coupons for a particular item, with the intent of using them all at once when the product goes on sale.

Acquire Coupons from the Internet. When many of us think of coupons, we think of the paper coupons that come attached to our favorite newspapers. While this is a tried-and-true method of saving money, there exists an additional avenue that a shopper can use to acquire coupons—the Internet. Simply select your coupons, print them out, and take them down to the local grocery store. If you are not sure where to start looking for online coupons, here is a list of some popular coupon websites, and you will find more listed on my website:

› Coupons.com

› CouponCabin.com

› CouponMom.com

› RetailMeNot.com

› SmartSource.com

It also bears mentioning that many retailers announce new sales on their Facebook accounts. If you Facebook regularly, you might consider adding some well-known grocers to your friend list.

Let Coupons Determine Dinner (and Other Meals). This is a really easy one. If you come across an excellent deal for pasta, whip up a pasta dish for dinner. Should you see a coupon offering a "Buy 1 Get 1 Free" special for tuna, plan on having a tuna sandwich for lunch. Essentially, try to plan your future meals based on the coupons you collect from various sources.

Be Organized. While virtually no one disputes the effectiveness and usefulness of coupons, many shoppers are wary about storing them. Indeed, many of us have trouble organizing our belongings and can easily envision ourselves losing a particular coupon among stacks of other coupons. This is where a coupon folder could prove very helpful. First, purchase an expandable folder (these folders are often used for keeping track of various tax documents). Second, divide this folder into specific sections, much the way you probably once divided your folders for school. For example, try creating separate sections for snacks, meats, fruits, veggies, or coupons set to expire in the immediate future. You could also try attaching related coupons using paper clips.

Join the Club. A number of retailers offer membership in "shopping clubs," complete with their very own card. This is a great way to save time, especially for those who loathe spending time clipping or printing out coupons. Once you join the club, place the club's card on your key ring or in your wallet. While ringing up your groceries, the cashier simply swipes the card, and the various grocery savings are added automatically to your purchases. Not only does this method require little effort on the part of the consumer, it can also yield big dividends, to the tune of 30 to 50 percent off in total savings. *Always* scan your card, and you will save a substantial amount of money over the course of a year. These clubs also apply to places like Subway, local establishments, and some big-box pet stores. So, it is not just groceries.

Fully Utilize Your Membership Card. Increasingly, grocers are encouraging shoppers to download coupons for various products directly onto their membership cards. To take advantage of this technology—as a consumer—you simply have to log on to the grocer's website (using your card's ID number), and load virtual coupons to your card. The coupon is activated once a cashier swipes the card at the grocery store.

Be Smart with Your Smart Phone. Is there anything that smartphones can't do? Software applications, known as apps, now exist that enable you to save additional money on groceries. In short, these apps act as membership cards on your phone, allowing you to ditch the additional plastic and still reduce your grocery bill.

Be Aware of Price Reductions. It's a little-known secret, but many supermarkets will cut the prices on perishable goods as they approach their sell-by dates. If you time things right, you can even combine a price reduction with a coupon. Now, this is also something that people need to pay attention to. If you are living in survival mode, you can go to your local grocer and ask them if they have groceries that are at their sell date, and many times they will give you the food. The best way to use this technique is to approach a store manager and explain your situation. Some stores may be hesitant to do this due to liability issues, but there are a lot of things like bread, cheese, and pasta that have sell-by dates that are perfectly consumable and will keep you and your family fed.

Don't Forget Lists. There's nothing wrong with resorting to old-school methods for saving money. Before you head out shopping, make a list of all the coupons you plan on using during your trip. This will help ensure that you don't forget to take advantage of, say, that coupon for laundry detergent. There are many free apps that can help with this, if you have a smartphone.

If It's Cheap, Buy a Lot of It. Suppose you stumble upon a super offer for toothpaste—buy two tubes for the price of one. Instead of buying just two containers, think about purchasing four, or even six. By the time you need toothpaste again, there is a good chance that toothpaste will once again be on sale.

Clear Out the Clearance Section. A store's clearance section is often full of items that stores are practically begging consumers to buy. In order to entice consumers to take these products off their hands, many retailers further reduce the already marked-down prices of clearance goods by offering coupon deals.

Make the Most out of Grocery Shopping. When possible, try stockpiling goods for about a one-month period. This will cut down on the number of trips you make to the grocery store, saving you both time and money in the process.

INDEX

Y

Z

ABOUT THE AUTHOR

Born in February 1975, Michael Anthony Sciucco, a.k.a. Michael Alden, grew up in Beverly, Massachusetts, where he struggled as a young child to follow the correct path in life. Through the years, Michael was fortunate to learn strategies and techniques that helped him develop a career path that removed him from a life surrounded by crime, drugs, and violence.

In 1997, Michael graduated from Springfield College with a degree in political science and went on to graduate from Suffolk University Law School in 2003, where he spent three out of the four years on the dean's list. Michael was general counsel of a large direct response firm for several years and, in 2009, founded Blue Vase Marketing, LLC, a premier direct response marketing firm, where he employs close to 150 people and is expanding his business internationally. Blue Vase Marketing, with an impressive 225 percent growth rate, was ranked by *Inc.* magazine as one of America's fastest growing companies in its 500/5000 list for 2013. His company continues to grow and is poised to be the most respected, powerful, and successful direct response firm in the world. Michael is also a host of *The Alden Report*, which airs all across the globe, discussing the benefits of various products and services. Michael holds several other formal licenses and has also authored publications about the direct response and health and wellness industries.

Want more? Visit AskMore-GetMore.com!